The Use of
AUDIO-VISUALS
in the Church

the
use of
AUDIO-
VISUALS
in the
church

OSCAR J. RUMPF

Illustrated by Anna R. Atene

THE CHRISTIAN EDUCATION PRESS
Philadelphia

PRINTED IN U.S.A. BY
SOWERS PRINTING CO., LEBANON, PA.

Dedicated to

My Mother and My Father

whose devotion to the church

was far-reaching

Acknowledgments

❦ ❦ THIS BOOK came into being over a period of years. It began to grow in pastorates in Kansas City and Sedalia, Missouri, and Hubbard, Iowa, where young people preparing for church membership, classes in leadership education and Sunday church school, groups in organizations and the congregations were the "guinea pigs" for much more experimentation than we then realized. The book continued to grow through the last twelve years in association with staff members of the Christian education units of the Evangelical and Reformed Church and the Congregational Christian Churches, and the staff members of Protestant denominations working in audio-visual workshops and conferences under the auspices of the Division of Christian Education and the Broadcasting and Film Commission of the National Council of Churches.

I am indebted to the assistant directors of the Bureau of Audio-Visual Aids of the Evangelical and Reformed Church, Luella C. Nieman and Helen C. Williams; and to the staff of the Bureau, Katherine Scholl, Elizabeth Kern, Evelyn Lambert, Doris Taylor, Naomi Steele, Alice Eshbach, Frank Greenwood, Arthur Williams, and Theodore Lepo, whose extra efforts in behalf of the Bureau allowed me time to plan and write.

Readers of early manuscripts or portions of them who made many helpful suggestions include the following: Mr. and Mrs. Herbert Graf, Mrs. Eugene W. Boch, Dorothea Pflug, Ethel Shellenberger, Mrs. W. Jack Banks, Professor Ernest F. Nolte. Bernice Buehler and Carolyn Goddard made many specific suggestions for improving the manuscript.

I am especially grateful to Dorothy Kloppe for her contribution toward the readability of the manuscript and to Herman Ahrens, Jr., for suggestions of some chapter titles and for his critical reading of early chapters.

The first manuscript for this book was typed from rather illegible notes by Alice Eshbach, my secretary in the Bureau of Audio-Visual Aids. The final manuscript was typed by my wife Alethea, who assisted in the development and writing in so many ways that her name should also appear as author.

Expressions of gratitude would not be complete without my mentioning specifically how much I owe to the thousands of rank and file members of the Evangelical and Reformed Church whose generous interest and support of the church provided me with the opportunity to grow.

Finally I wish to pay special tribute to the late Alan Shilin for his contribution to my thinking through approximately ten years of our association in the planning, writing, and production of films and filmstrips.

Oscar J. Rumpf

Webster Groves, Missouri
January, 1958

Contents

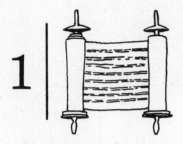

We Have a Story to Tell

❧ ❧ JESUS is central to all history. Events before and after his birth are dated by him. No other man has so radically altered men's lives. He has reached lower for men and lifted them higher than any other man in history. No individual or nation has been able to refute his word. His teachings have been unexcelled, his life unequaled. Jesus of Nazareth is the greatest single event in history.

We who represent the Christian church have him as our heritage and our example. We who are teachers and leaders, pastors and ministers, have his story to tell, to transmit, to communicate. We are charged with the responsibility of helping persons understand and accept this man and his message. We want others to know, understand, and believe in Jesus Christ. We want them to grow and be nurtured as Christians. We want persons, ourselves included, to know, understand, and have faith in him and all he means, to the end that their lives and ours will be changed. We want to change, and we want people to change, to follow him, to be like him. Remember, he was the most important man in history. His message is unsurpassed, his mission unexcelled. With such a message, mission, and resource our teaching ought not fail or falter. And yet it does. We have a

1

story to tell that often is inadequately told. We fail to communicate clearly.

Jesus' message transformed millions not only because it was true but also because it was transmitted. Hearers understood it. He taught less than three years. His sources? First-hand experience and the oral and written record of his people. His methods? Storytelling . . . painting pictures with parables. He communicated.

The message and the mission of the Christian church are the same today as they were in New Testament times. It is our responsibility to make them known. We too can and must communicate. This age of sight and sound, of mechanics and electronics, of great knowledge and endless horizons, has given us projection and recording equipment, screens and lighting, three-dimensional color pictures and stereophonic sound. It has provided us with a wealth of communication facilities. But it has not changed our message or our mission.

The message and the mission of the church are the same, save for those necessary variations which we have had to make to meet the needs of our times. The means by which we communicate our message, however, have changed, must change. The methods of our mission have altered, must alter.

One day our five-year-old son, Bob, and his mother caught a mouse in a trap. As they were coming down the stairs with it Bob asked his mother to show it to his one-year-old brother.

When his mother objected, saying that they could not tell little brother about it because he would not understand, five-year-old Bob countered with the words, "You don't have to tell him about it; just show it to him."

Telling, by itself, has had its day. Showing is coming into its own. We still need to tell, but we also need to show. In fact, we need to do much more by way of communication, and audio-visuals will help us to do it. Audio-visuals will augment, complement, and supplement our teaching.

The children, young people, and adults of our churches live in a world that has almost become "one," and in an age that communicates rapidly and readily. Life is now filled with sights and sounds from everywhere. We have touched people and tasted products from all over the earth. Our culture has conditioned us to see, hear, taste, smell, and touch. The world we live in is an audio-visual world.

Our business as educators, communicators, witnesses of the gospel of Jesus Christ is to make that gospel better known, more widely understood and more universally accepted. And we want it to come alive in people. Competition is stiff, to say the least.

Our task is carried on in an age that clamors, from many sides, for the attention and interest of those we seek to reach. School, business, government, social institutions are using mass communication media. When the world about us educates by electronics, the Christian church must use more than candlelight. A bedlam of sights and sounds are bombarding the eyes and ears of people. Scores of voices compete with the voice of the church and the church school. Do we understand what this competition is doing to our program of reaching persons? Our sounds and scenes must be clear, organized, purposeful, and distinctive. There is more and more to know in this twentieth century, and thus there is more and more to communicate. Our experiences, and correspondingly our responsibilities, have been multiplied a hundredfold.

We do not propose that in using audio-visuals in the church we resort to any method or mass communication procedure that comes along. We do suggest that the church carefully examine the media available, to determine what will help us to do our job better.

Nor are we advocating that the church set up a special audio-visual program of using films and filmstrips in and for themselves. Some churches did, and still do, schedule and show films once a month without regard to the needs of persons or the purposes of the church. A men's group in the church may want to see a recreation film or a social action film or a Bible film as they plan their program. But the men's group does not exist and should not exist just to be entertained. The purposes of church-directed organizations are usually higher than that.

The church should have no audio-visual program as such. The church has the same message and mission it has always had. Audio-visuals will help us communicate and carry on that program; they will make clear, real, and effective our message and our mission. But they should neither dominate, determine, nor supplant the program of the church.

4

The mechanics we have used have not always been matched by high quality materials or a mind-set geared to proper and adequate utilization. Sometimes our machines have become more important than our messages. Sometimes a film has displaced a teacher, disrupted a relationship, destroyed an opportunity.

Allen O. Miller has written in his book, *Invitation to Theology*,[1] these words: "The awesome task of communicating the love and righteousness of God from one generation to another, and at the same time of exemplifying that love and righteousness as the life and mission of the people of God, defines nothing less than the entire function of the Christian church." He goes on to say, "A serious study of human communication must maintain a clear distinction between two different forms or types: (1) transmission through verbal or sensory symbols, and (2) communion through participation in personal encounter. Both forms of communication are important. Neither is to be discredited nor adjudged inadequate to its purpose. By the same token neither can do the job of the other, for each operates in different spheres of knowledge."

All of us who are concerned with the use of audio-visuals should bear in mind the discerning truth contained in Dr. Miller's book. For we have a tendency to become communicators of less than the best, the more we fail to have communion with him who is our Lord. Our failures often stem not from defective methods or media but from the lack of spiritual resources to share with our brothers. The more we cut ourselves off from our basic spiritual resource, communion with God, the less able we will be to communicate with our children or our brothers. It is important and necessary for us to examine our failures if we are to tell the Christian story well.

Communication failures of those of us who teach in church

---

[1] Published by The Christian Education Press.

schools have been a major factor wherever there are losses in enrollment and attendance. When teenagers say, "It's not interesting," "All he does is talk," and "The place is dead," they are talking about communication failures. When children sit between blank walls and disregard a teacher who reads from a lesson quarterly there is a communication failure. When adults submit unwittingly to a weekly church school "preaching lecture" or a sermon without action, reaction, or interaction, communication has failed. We are not getting through.

In planning to tell our story better and more widely, pastors, teachers, and leaders of the church must be aware of the opportunity audio-visuals afford. We will need to recognize where we are and how far we have come in making use of these media. We must ask and answer questions like these: How interested are we in communicating a message, in changing persons, in fulfilling a mission? Will the teaching techniques presently employed by the church stand up in competition with the communication techniques that are used all about us in the world outside the church school? Even if we should disregard the fact that others outside the church are using audio-visual media, are we not under obligation to reach persons and nurture them as Christians by employing the best means that we know? Can the church afford to teach less effectively than the school or business? When children, young people, and adults are taught with the rich resources of audio-visuals in the schools of the nation, how will they feel about the church and church school program where fewer, if any, audio-visuals are used and where the teacher still "tells" the lesson? What is our responsibility in communicating the message and carrying out the mission of the church of Jesus Christ?

Our business, as teachers, is communication. We know that rich experience, concrete experience, is the best basis for all understanding. All that the eyes can see or the ears can hear, and everything that impinges on the other senses, are truly audio-

6

visuals, aids to instruction. Providing these for our pupils—by the use of all media now available—is our task.

The teacher is communication personified. From the pupil's point of view the teacher is the message and the mission. Do you remember with any accuracy very much of what you were taught in church school classes? I cannot! But I do remember every teacher who taught me for any considerable length of time. He or she was what I learned. He or she was the audio-visual. The experience was good, but it could have been richer and more concrete. The teacher can never be replaced by any audio-visual, but audio-visual materials used by a well-prepared teacher will greatly enrich the experience of pupils. Pupil participation will increase. There will be much more work for the teacher, but it will be more effective work and more interesting. Preparing to teach will take more time, but teaching time will be more fruitful.

We are communicators. We have something precious and important to communicate. We have pupils with whom we wish to communicate. Together we will plan for rich and concrete experiences. In this communications world we will lay plans for the use of audio-visuals.

Audio-visuals had their beginning in the Christian church when parables were painted with words, writing was done in the sand, and Christian secret meetings were announced by the signs of the fish and the cross. Early Christians had few if any painted pictures; so they painted their own in imagination. The sounds they made to express their feelings were the sounds of the voice in talking and simplified singing, or those created with crudely fashioned musical instruments. But the use of audio-visuals grew.

Through these almost twenty centuries of the Christian era much use has been made of audio-visuals. Men who could not read words could "read" windows. When men could not read the scriptures or the writings of the saints, symbols and images of saints and their teachings were brought near and set up in glass, paintings, mosaics, marble, and stone. The life of Jesus and his disciples, the teachings of Jesus and the history of the church, were placed in full view and preached and sung so they could be heard. Audio-visuals are not new to the Christian church. Certain audio-visuals are new, and the uses to which we put all of them are on the increase.

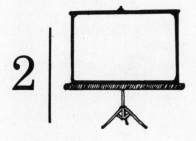

2

What Do Audio-Visuals Do for Us?

❧ ❧ Audio-visuals are useful. We no longer need to prove their value in the program of the church. We have such proof available from the use made of them by schools, business, the armed forces, and the church. Today audio-visuals are used with all ages, from the nursery child to the university graduate.

In this chapter we shall attempt to state fifteen specific functions which audio-visuals may perform, to answer the question: What do audio-visuals do for us? They may perform more than one of these functions at a time and could conceivably perform almost all of them at one time.

Audio-visuals condense time and space. They squeeze time and fasten events together. They bridge gaps in history. They function as a See-It-Now program. A film about Jesus shows him living now. A three-foot map reduces a distance of thousands of miles to a few inches—to within the realm of comprehension. Then Palestine is not so far away. A filmstrip on church history or the life of Christ reduces the time span and links events together.

Audio-visuals teach skills. They present ideas in sequence.

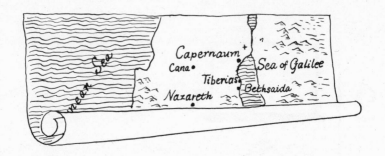

They give content to an idea through a visual concept. They provide unity. A series of still pictures will teach skills by presenting the steps singly and in sequence. A demonstration of how to tie a knot will clarify that difficult feat for the tenderfoot. Watching a person tie the knot and then following his example step by step is the most concrete way to learn knottieing. The film *Wet Mounting Pictorial Materials*,[1] on how to wet mount pictures, equips a viewer to perform this task intelligently.

Audio-visuals transmit knowledge. They instruct. They reduce ambiguity. They present information in an interesting way. They answer the questions of *what, how,* and *when.* They equip a viewer and listener to perform his duties intelligently. A film like *Our Bible—How It Came to Us* gives information, transmits knowledge. Scribes and copyists are seen at work. Lan-

---

[1] Produced by Indiana University, Bloomington, Indiana.

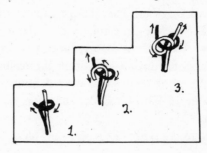

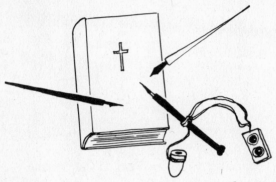

guages in which the Bible came to us are seen in the process of being written down.

Audio-visuals stimulate thought. They bring complex human situations into the classroom for analysis. They cause us to ask questions. The film *Boundary Lines* is such an audio-visual. It asks, "What is a line anyway, except what we make it? A line can mean water, or mountain, or tree, or man. A line can mean light, or love, or yes, or no, or perhaps; for a line speaks any language, and this line could mean many things—ball, or balloon, or the whole wide world. You see, a line is what we make it because a line is only an idea." One idea triggers another idea. Thinking takes place when the mind is occupied with some subject—when ideas revolve in the mind, when we muse, meditate, and cogitate upon a subject.

Audio-visuals motivate us to take action. They prompt and precipitate us to study, work, give, understand, and worship. They instigate action. They stimulate the will. They push and pull at our hearts and minds until we want to be like what we see. *The Guest, No Greater Power,* and *The Secret of the Gift* are films that motivate us to share and give. A film like *Barabbas the Robber* would motivate us to understand, really understand, what is meant by the exclamation, "He died for me!"

Audio-visuals make things real. They tie things to our own experience. They cause us to say, "It happened, even if it was only once." "Now I can believe. I've seen it!" They give evi-

dence that makes things concrete. Doubt is removed. One can see and touch things. Models come in this category, but the most real audio-visual is the object or experience itself. One can make or purchase a small scroll, but it is far more educational to go to a Jewish synagogue and hold the scroll in one's hands, see the actual writing, know its weight and how to roll and unroll it. If one made and transcribed a scroll it would be even more real. A good motion picture film on the life of Jesus is the most real way to present the story of Jesus to those who have never heard of him or know little about him.

Audio-visuals give form to words, phrases, and imaginings. They enrich experience. They correct misconceptions. The Jordan River seen on a slide or on motion picture film becomes more than a beautiful blue river running straight from the Sea of Galilee to the Dead Sea. It is now known to be like other rivers—winding, narrowing, widening, and muddy. It isn't really like the bath water we draw from a tap, or like the water in a blue lake on a clear day.

Audio-visuals provide a setting. They orient us to new situations. They create an atmosphere. They provide a learning situation. They give us moorings. They answer the question *where.* A flat picture of some merit can help create a beautiful worship center. Flat wall maps help us locate cities, rivers, and mountains. A relief map is more useful because the model is more real. All other factors being equal, a film on *Ruth,* much of it done in Palestine, provides a more accurate setting for the story than one done in the hills around Hollywood, California. *Decision in Hong Kong* establishes without any doubt that this kind of "community" is composed of hills with hovels and the homeless, and streets with riches and rags.

Audio-visuals show relationships. They link together. They indicate degree. They allow for ready comparison. We can compare the known to the unknown. They enable us to make comparisons with ourselves, with others, with things. We can com-

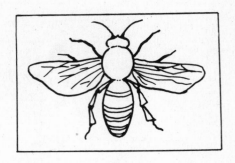

pare size, shape, effect. Graphs, charts, and time lines are used to show relationships.

Audio-visuals enlarge what is too small so one may see it clearly. They reduce the size of the large items and make them visible, comprehensible. They slow down what is too fast. They capture and hold fast the fleeting moment, the impression, the feeling, and in a sense something of the eternal. They speed up, into a matter of minutes or even seconds, a process that ordinarily takes weeks. *God's Wonders in Flowers* presents by time-lapse photography the growth of a flower. The filmstrip *Wonders of God* enlarges a bee to make clear how uniquely God has equipped this small creature.

Audio-visuals increase and heighten interest. A color chart on a bulletin board gets our attention. A cartoon interests a child. He may pass up a church school story paper for it. Television shows that run the gamut in the use of audio-visuals almost do obeisance to "the hook." "The hook" refers to the interest catcher. Every good audio-visual has (or puts) such a hook on the viewer-listener. Even the subject of audio-visuals, such as plays a secondary part in the film *Thursday's Children,* catches our interest.

Audio-visuals aid group work. When the group is large we speak in terms of a mass. We call audio-visuals mass media of communication, though the church's best use will usually involve mostly small groups. They create a unity, a feeling of one-

ness. They easily establish an *esprit de corps*, a groupness. The use of audio-visuals provides the group with something of the same background. They have a common denominator. The class starts off together on the basis of a common experience.

Audio-visuals make possible satisfying, aesthetic experiences. They provide a sense of pleasure and of enjoyment. They lift the spirit, stimulate the emotions, set the mind at ease on a higher level. A recording of Bach's *B minor Mass* will cause the spirit to soar and release a man from the mundane. A film on the life of a noble person will pull us outside ourselves to something higher. It will bring our incomplete drives and our unfulfilled dreams closer together.

Audio-visuals reinforce or channel ideas which help persons to change their attitudes. Seeing is believing. A racially prejudiced man, seeing the film *The Color of a Man*, agreed that the differ-

ences between races which he had thought lay deeper were merely a matter of skin pigmentation and lack of opportunity. An objective cartoon-style filmstrip like *Is Your Home Fun?* where the Gays and the Browns are seen in contrast, helps viewer-listeners to see themselves and laugh at themselves, thus channeling ideas that make for a change in family relationships. Audio-visuals can marshal facts, portray events, establish situations, and present them so interestingly that the old beliefs, old ideas are uprooted and replaced by the factual, the logical, the believable, the new, and the more inclusive.

Audio-visuals help us to concentrate. They save time. Projected audio-visuals usually do this best. Shades are drawn, the room is darkened, and the picture is projected on the screen.

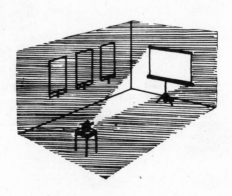

There is nowhere else to look except within. The situation forces concentration. However, a good audio-visual will cause us to concentrate even if there is a subdued light, if room lights are turned down only slightly. Man is visually constituted. Eighty-five per cent of his learning is done through his eyes. Audio-visuals hold attention. They pull the eye in the direction of the concrete. They tune in on the ear. When sight and sound are well integrated in a film or filmstrip, viewer concentration takes place. Audio-visuals save time. *I Beheld His Glory* is a 55-minute color film that tells the story of Jesus from the triumphal entry to the resurrection. Imagine, if you can, how long it would take a teacher to *tell* the detailed facts of this story to a group of senior highs, and how impossible it would be for him to provide the great overtones and undertones of the symphony of sight and sound that are present in the film.

3

Some Problems to Solve

🙟🙟 🙟🙟 THREE MAJOR PROBLEMS related to communication confront the Christian church. They are the unfamiliarity of the ancient source of our faith and life, over-emphasis on tradition in form, and verbalism.

We have inherited the Christian faith and way of life from an ancient source. Much of the church's teaching, life, and work are based on three years in the life of one man who lived two thousand years ago. Two thousand years seem like a long time ago to persons in our era. Our basic record and resource is the Bible, which came from ancient times. It is not easy to read the Bible nor to understand what it says. The language is not always clear. Many of the everyday activities of Bible people are unfamiliar to us. Their thought patterns and ours differ greatly. Moreover, the Bible comes to us from the pens of persons who made mistakes. The faith and life of the Christian church come to us from an ancient source which is not without error and which is often difficult to understand.

The conserving nature of religion is both positive and negative in effect. It is the nature of religion to hold on to what has been revealed and what has been taught by precept and example. When religion has got hold of something valuable in the way

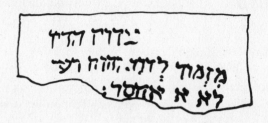

of truth it has sought to preserve it. We record such revelations
of truth in order to have them for ourselves and to transmit
them to new converts and future generations. Much of religion
is promulgated through conservation. Peter said on the Mount
of Transfiguration, "Master, it is well that we are here; let us
make three booths" (Mark 9:5). However, there is a tendency
for us to conserve not only truth but the forms in which truth is
transmitted. Old forms become sacred, but they may and do
become meaningless and obsolete. When our religion calls upon
us to conserve both truth and the manner of receiving and trans-
mitting truth, then it follows logically that we question every
new method and procedure, especially if they have anything to
do with religion.

In earlier days some churches were violently opposed to the
use of sound motion pictures for two basic reasons: First,
churches showing films were thought to be following the ways
of the world; and second, it was felt religion was supposed to be
"taught" and preached, meaning given by word of mouth.
Others opposed their use because it involved us in disobedience
of the second Commandment, for we were thought to be makers
and worshipers of images (pictures).

Tradition in form is important, but sometimes the way something is said or done becomes a substitute for the element of
truth conveyed by the saying and the doing. Ways of doing
things become sacred in and of themselves long after the reasons for doing them are forgotten. Purposes are lost sight of

through monotonous and unvaried repetition. The way one holds a cup and the manner in which one partakes of bread have often taken precedence over the meaning a cup and bread originally had for Christians. The use of vestments and robes often exalts the clergy and choir, whereas robing was done originally to keep man from calling attention to himself, to make men better able to exalt God only.

Through the centuries the church has developed certain forms of operation that have become traditional and are good. Rites are performed according to specific patterns. Church organization makes for continuity. But rites, forms, and procedures can get in the way of new revelations of truth, in the way of progress. Thus we teach as our fathers taught and as we were taught. We employ the same patterns, forms, and words without regard to the situation or need that produced them. The new age and the new situation are approached with old methods. It was Jesus himself who said, "New wine is put into fresh wineskins." Many traditional procedures are valuable and necessary to the life of the church. Frequently, though, we do things in the church in a certain way not because it is the best way, the most educational, or the quickest, but because we have always done things that way. The church has not often enough re-examined its teaching methods and procedures, its policies and programs.

Protestant Christianity has always stood strongly for preaching the Word. Preaching and teaching can, and often have, become mere verbalizing. Words sometimes lack meaning for the speaker and also for the listener. Verbalism is defined by Webster as: (1) an empty form of words; (2) wordiness. Too often we use words taken out of their usual context, words from an ancient source, abstract words, words whose meaning we have failed to investigate. Hearing words of scripture read can be a meaningless jumble of sound unless we know their meaning and they are read with understanding. Words like Savior, calvary, atonement, gospel, blood of the Lamb, and Lamb slain for

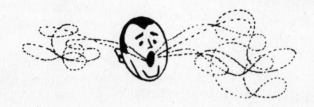

us are useless with persons whose experiences are not sufficiently concrete to enable them to grasp their meaning.

Talk has been our stock in trade. When our talk is about something unrelated to our experiences, out of a little understood ancient time, about an ancient book that is not easy to read, concerning a person we have never met, we are to some extent involved in verbalism. Edgar Dale says, "Verbalism is a disease caught in school." Actually, it is only a symptom. The disease is more deep-seated—it is lack of understanding, lack of experience. But it can be cured.

It would be a shocking revelation to a great many of us teachers, pastors, and Christian educators if we discovered the meanings persons attached to frequently used words. A number of regular church and church school members were asked to tell what they first pictured or thought of when they heard the words given below. As you will note, some of the answers were correct, but a number were incorrect. Most misconceptions could have been avoided through the use of audio-visuals. You may want to conduct a similar test with the group you teach. If you do, be sure to state very clearly that you want to know the first picture each word conjures up in their minds. The persons with whom we conducted the test answered as follows:

Palestinian house—stone house, cave, mud hut (no roof, sit on floor), tent, clay house, small.

Nomad—shepherd, people roving the countryside, didn't know.

Jordan River—dirty water like all rivers, clear blue where people were baptized, wide, straight, more of a clear-water stream, blue.

Wilderness—jumble of stuff, can't get through, sand and rocks, no habitation, woods, hills, pasture, not dense foliage.

Thieves and robbers—scantily dressed, poor and sneaky, arrogant, bands of them, robbed travelers, break in and steal, dressed poor like in rags, stole because they didn't have anything.

Synagogue—spacious room, people with turbans sitting on floor, fire burning, money being exchanged, gambling taking place, stone building, large building, like their houses not large.

Shepherd—boy Joseph, dirty men, food scarce, lived in caves, clothes dirty, wore turban and used staff, had a dog, rugged men, bearded like a farmer, clothed in skins, took care of sheep, not too much clothing, uncultured.

The misconceptions noted in these descriptions resulted to some extent from verbalism. The persons answering described what came to mind on the basis of what they had heard, not what they had experienced. None had been to Palestine. Only one remembered a picture of the Jordan, another remembered seeing the picture, "Arrival of the Shepherds," by Lerolle. The rest spoke out of their own experience here in the United States and what they had been taught in church and church school. All had pictured the Jordan as a straight river running from the Sea of Galilee to the Dead Sea. Only a few thought it was muddy water. For some it was blue like the water in one of our Great Lakes. The use of Kodachrome slides on the land of Palestine would have helped to clear up such misconceptions. Adding and multiplying experiences through the use of audio-visuals would have helped to reduce the amount of verbalism with which the students were saturated. The answers they gave revealed to some extent how much of what we preach and teach is mere verbalism.

We have a rich heritage upon which we can draw and to which we contribute. We have a responsibility under God to transmit it. This is difficult unless we make it our own. In so doing, we need to re-examine, redefine, and restate our faith. We need to make clear and real what is ancient and unknown. We need to enrich the experience of our church people by the use of all the media that we can afford and can use well in the program of the church.

4

Thirty-two Ways to
Tell a Story

❧ ❧ THERE ARE MANY audio-visual resources available to
the church school teacher. They range from words to objects,
from the abstract to the concrete. Words may tell us about a
Palestinian house, but words alone cannot make the concept of
that house as clear and as memorable to the hearer as can a
small model of the house. The details of such a house are
clearer if the pupil sketches it, makes a model out of clay, or
carves it out of soap. There is no substitute in learning for the
experience of living in a Palestinian home. Experience is still
the best teacher. But since direct experience is not always possible, teaching by the use of audio-visual resources is the next
best thing.

A lesson is taught when it is learned. A lesson may be taught
with words. But it will be more interesting and be remembered
longer if the leader uses audio-visual resources to give it experi-
ential learning values. What resources could one use? Let us
illustrate by listing the more frequently used audio-visual resources in teaching the following information to a class of junior
boys and girls.

*Jesus lived more than 1900 years ago in Palestine, a land
that was only forty-five miles wide and ninety miles long. He*

was born in a manger in Bethlehem. His parents were named Joseph and Mary. Joseph was a carpenter. Jesus grew up in Nazareth. Joseph and Mary, his parents, taught him much about God. Jesus called God "Father," "Our Father."

1. WORDS

Printed or written words are visual symbols. They stand for something. The primitives of every land on the globe first wrote with pictures. Then those pictures were shortened into symbols, and later the symbols were united into words and sentences. When words are uttered by the human voice, they form articulate sounds that express ideas. A word, printed or uttered, holds meaning for the reader or hearer in direct proportion to the experience he has had with the idea in back of it. A word is abstract, the object or person it represents is concrete. The word "house" is abstract. The house itself is real.

The words printed above in our lesson for juniors are a visualization. They tell a brief story. They are understandable to most juniors in our church schools. But just because they are understood is no proof that they will be remembered, especially since they have been presented in only one form. Repetition is one of the best ways to learn. Let us see how the lesson can be made more meaningful and more memorable.

2. DIAGRAM

A diagram is an illustrative figure that shows relationships and outlines. It is graphic in nature and assists in explaining facts. The public school teaches geometry by the use of diagrams. Dress patterns and simple outline maps are diagrams.

A diagram on a chalkboard could picture Jesus' parents and the contribution each made to the life and thought of Jesus. This could be shown in two columns of equal length, and would help juniors see the importance of two parents in the life of every child.

25

3. TIME LINE

A time line is a drawn line on paper or chalkboard accurately marked to scale with dates of major events. One may also use a string or a clothesline and clothespins to hold paper bearing dates. One or more of the dates should already have been a part of the experience of the viewers. Relative lengths of time are thus depicted. No matter what one uses, nor what periods of history are marked off on the time line, it should not include too much. The time line is one of the simplest of audio-visuals to construct. It should be readily intelligible. Time lines help answer the questions: How long? When? In what relationship?

A time line would give junior children some conception of when Jesus was born in relationship to other important historical events. A horizontal line could be drawn on a chalkboard representing 33 years' time. At the extreme left a short vertical line could represent the dividing time between B.C. and A.D. and should be so indicated. As many vertical lines as are needed could be drawn in their proper places across the horizontal line to date the main events in Jesus' early life. One may use only dates, such as 6 B.C. and A.D. 30, or one may also add other visuals such as drawings and flat pictures. A series of junior-age activities visualizing some of the things we do that are similar to what Jesus did to help his mother and father could be cut out or drawn by the children in church school. Pictures of children at work could be cut out of magazines.

4. CHART OR GRAPH

A chart is a graphic presentation exhibiting information by the use of bars, pies, or figures. There are time charts, tree or stream charts, and comparison charts.

The bar chart is used most commonly. Let us assume that one bar chart represents the life span of Jesus. The bar may be divided into three ten-year periods, and another bar representing a ten-year-old junior child's life span placed above or below it. The junior child will then have a better idea of how long Jesus lived because he will see Jesus' life span in comparison with his own.

The Christian church, with all its various branches, is sometimes depicted by a tree chart.

To indicate the relative size of the land of Palestine in Jesus' day, one could cut out of paper, using the same scale, maps of the state in which one lives and of Palestine, alternately laying one over the other for comparison. Or pupils could show a comparison of the length and breadth of a map of the land of Palestine by making two charts scaled to miles, which could be placed over the map.

5. FRIEZE OR MURAL

A frieze is any longitudinal or horizontal series of pictures that tell a story. The pictures are usually pasted, pinned, or drawn on a roll of paper that is hung on a wall. A mural illustrates a single idea or subject by a series of pictures. It is usually thought of as a painting on a wall. The pictures for the frieze or mural may be assembled after the pupils have virtually completed a study. They are made out of a great number of resources to which the group has been introduced.

A series of pictures selected or drawn (or both) illustrating our paragraph would visualize the contents in sequence. The frieze or mural would help the pupils to see the events in order, in their proper setting, and would show their relationship.

The area where one will hang, tack, or paste the frieze needs to be selected before one begins, to insure having sufficient space. One long sheet of paper, cut into three sections, or a number of uniformly-sized large sheets may be used. The large sheets could be put together later. After the group has decided on the story to tell, responsibility could be assigned so that the complete story or idea will be visualized. Pictures may be sketched in lightly with light chalk which tempera paint will cover. All the practice sheets may be hung on a clothesline for everyone to see. Either tempera paints, crayolas, or water-color paints work well. The paint may be applied with brushes or by finger painting. For the final painting, the paper may be placed on the floor, the wall, or a proper-size table, depending upon which is the best surface. Each artist may wish to tell what his section of the mural means.

6. MAP OR GLOBE

A map is a representation, usually on a flat surface, of a part of the earth's surface or of the heavens. A globe presents a round representation of the world. Certain public schools have very large globes in special places for all to see. They use wall space, otherwise unused, on which to place large maps. Map makers usually place the country where the map is to be used in the center of the map. But when they make a globe, no nation is in the center—all are on the outside hanging on for dear life. The globe is the only adequate map in this age of space travel.

An outline map drawn on the chalkboard, or better still a full color map of Palestine showing Bethlehem, Jerusalem, Nazareth, and naming the Jordan River and the Sea of Galilee, will locate these places and natural resources in relationship to each other. The places and events in the life of Jesus will become real. They were a part of his world. They are a part of our world, for some are still in existence.

If maps are drawn by junior boys and girls, the children are more likely to remember the places and the events about which they are studying.

Youth and adult church school groups should have before them a set of maps of Palestine in Old and New Testament times. Maps are readily available today from a number of sources, such as bookstores and Friendship Press.

Juniors will want to make table maps, using a picture frame border, colored paper, and either papier-mâché or salt and flour paste. Their maps will picture the area of their concern—places they have visited, or mission lands, to which place markers may be attached for identification. Before sending a gift away, a picture of the gift or a label naming the recipient may be pinned on the spot to which it is going.

7. BULLETIN BOARD

A bulletin board, or tackboard, is a wall display constructed of soft composition board or cork to which various visuals such as graphs, pictures, and some objects may be tacked to present their message to viewers.

The boys and girls may draw small maps of Palestine, pictures of Palestinian homes, or the Bethlehem manger scene. These, along with cutouts from church school literature and magazines saved for the purpose, may be used to visualize a simple ten- to fifteen-picture story illustrating the lesson.

A bulletin board, as such, is not a visual, but it functions as a visual when it is orderly and adequately used for display, exhibit, and the dissemination of information. Every church can have one.

The following general principles will assist in using the bulletin board or tackboard:

» Keep it attractive with proper arrangement and color.

» Limit the number of visuals used.

» Maintain a balance, as to both visualization and content.

» Change the contents frequently.

» Ask one person to be responsible for the bulletin board, but enlist the help of artists and designers.

» If you have a central theme, make all other items support it.

» Use variety in color, form, placement, lettering, and drawings.

» Do not use it at all some Sundays. (Leave it beautifully blank occasionally.)

» Use a large question mark, and below it the words "Coming Next Week," to announce a big event.

8. POSTER

A poster is a cardboard wall hanging, usually not less than 12 x 16 inches in size, employing pictures or words or both.

A poster could be made concerning several portions of our lesson for juniors: Bethlehem at night, the manger scene, scenes of the birthplace and the boyhood travels of Jesus, Jesus learning from his parents, the meaning of the words "Our Father." When a person has thought through a subject sufficiently and made a good and intelligible poster of it, he will have learned much about that subject.

A poster must be of a size that can be easily seen by persons in the room farthest away, so arranged as to focus attention on the one idea or line of action it is intended to illustrate, and simple enough so that it can be taken in by a sustained glance.

Posters may be used to:

Illustrate a hymn

Illustrate a story

Make clear the meaning of Christian conduct

Motivate giving by a graphic presentation of need

Produce an atmosphere for a special day

Announce or interpret a special event or program

9. CHALKBOARD

A chalkboard is a flat surface (often light green) on which one can write or draw with various colors of chalk.

There are many ways to use the chalkboard. A list could be made of the things the boys and girls already know about Jesus. As indicated previously, it may be used for the time line, chart, or map. Or one could use the chalkboard for drawings made by the children.

Every room in the church except the nursery room should have a clean, well-kept chalkboard. Chalkboards come in several colors, and several colors of chalk will brighten the words or drawings as well as show contrasts. It would be well to have a three-foot ruler available for drawing straight lines. The chalkboard may be used to:

State the subject of a lesson

Present a lesson outline

Spell difficult words

Record pupil suggestions and list points made in the discussion

Draw symbols, diagrams, figures, time lines, and maps

List facts and figures

Make announcements

10. FLIP CHART

A flip chart is a number of large sheets of paper fastened together at one end to a tripod or stand at an angle of 20 or 30 degrees. One may write or draw on the chart and glue flat pictures to its surface. It may be prepared in advance or used as a chalkboard for writing salient points, making diagrams, or recording group findings or decisions. The recorded material may be transferred later to typewritten sheets or preserved as chart sheets. Using different colors of crayons, one can write or draw in such a way as to catch the eye and relate materials of a similar nature to each other.

Flip chart sheets may be purchased, or one can obtain newsprint and cut the sheets from it. The writing and drawing on a flip chart should be large enough to be seen by the person in the last row of seats. In turning a flip chart, one should stand to the right of the chart, facing the audience. The sheet should be grasped with the left hand at the bottom-right. Still facing the audience, the user lifts the chart sheet in a rolling fashion over the top of the chart stand in one single unhesitating motion. When this is practiced a few times the audience will be freed of any fear that the sheet will be torn in the "flipping" process.

The flip chart, with white sheets, may be used on a Sunday morning for making a special announcement and for the background and border of a flat picture. Small outline pictures, placed in an opaque projector and projected onto the chart sheet, may then be drawn on it by tracing over the lines with black or colored crayons.

Our story of Jesus could be outlined on several pages of the flip chart. One could also use the flip chart for a chalkboard and draw diagrams, time lines, and outline pictures of the lesson on it.

11. SKETCHES AND CARTOONS

Sketches and cartoons are hastily executed drawings presenting essential features of persons or things. Much thought usually precedes the execution of such sketches. Cartoons present a subject in a light or humorous vein.

All the children may be helped by sketching, on paper or chalkboard, a picture of persons and scenes they remember from their present learning and their past experience. The teacher and pupils may then study the sketches and make some comparison with library resources to stimulate thinking and insure greater accuracy.

Cartoons usually remind us of sketches in the daily newspaper or in magazines where persons are caricatured. But there are also symbolic cartoons that do not ridicule or caricature. Children will find it interesting and helpful to make such drawings of persons and animals, depicting the less serious aspects of our lesson. They may draw small animals by the manger, the boy Jesus playing with his pets or working with his father's tools. From these drawings the teacher may learn much about the pupils.

12. FLAT PICTURES

A flat picture, in black and white or color, can be used in worship or teaching. It may be framed and hung on a wall or placed on an easel. A flat picture in a frame is referred to as a framed picture.

The picture file of an orderly church school department will contain a great variety of color drawings, received with church school materials in previous years, on the birth and life of Jesus. One picture may be set up in the worship center and others may be thumbtacked (or made to adhere by using a sticky gummed substance) on the bulletin board. Or they may be used by the teacher, who will place them on an easel or hold them before the class to illustrate various aspects of the lesson such as the manger scene; Jesus, Joseph, and Mary in their home; Jesus and Joseph in the carpenter shop; or a Palestinian family in their home.

13. KAMISHABI

The kamishabi originated in Japan. It is a series of uniform-size flat pictures placed together and held in a vertical position on a table or stand visible to a small group. The number of pictures used is dependent on the availability of the pictures and the content of the story. The sizes may vary but are approximately 15 x 20 inches. The storyteller interprets the front picture by reading off the back of the last picture. The procedure is to remove the first picture from the front to the rear. The back of the first picture contains the story of the second picture.

Pictures on the subject of our study, selected from primary and junior picture sets, could be used to make a kamishabi. The juniors are to think through the story of each picture and write a script. The script, written large and legibly, should be pasted or attached by other means to the back of the preceding picture. Kamishabi are in common use with kindergarten children in

Japan. But children of other lands and other ages are equally interested in "seeing-hearing" a story via the kamishabi.

14. PICTUROL

A picturol is a series of pictures pasted or drawn on a roll of paper, the ends of which are fastened to two sticks. One may make a picturol by placing a grocery box on its side and inserting sections of a broom handle through the top and bottom of the box, about three inches from the sides and front. The two ends of the roll of paper may be fastened to the two sticks, and the paper rolled up on the stick to the right as one faces the box. Then the other stick should be turned slowly, with the paper moving from picture to picture. The children may wish to tell the story as the pictures are viewed. Sometimes the reading of a written narration accompanies the showing of the pictures.

This medium calls for class participation in choosing the pictures. The children may be asked to look for pictures and bring them to the church school. It is best to gather all the pictures available and place them in a simple file under very general headings. When the story or idea is jelled, the children may be asked to select the pictures they will use. They may trim the pictures and place them in order on the roll of paper, marked off with numbers as to where they should be placed. The pictures may also be placed on sheets of paper and fastened together with glue, Scotch tape, or paper staples.

A series of pictures cut out or drawn, and pasted in sequence on a roll of paper by the children, will be their "motion picture." It is a "motion picture" when they move it to the next scene, and each scene becomes a still picture when the motion stops. The pupils will write their own script or tell the story in their own words. Such a picturol with story will provide a logically connected account, readily understandable and made possible through the purposeful and meaningful activity of the class.

15. OPAQUE PROJECTOR

The opaque projector is a device with mirrors and a special system of lenses for projecting materials (flat pictures, printed matter, and small objects less than 10 x 10 inches in size) onto a screen.

It is normal and helpful for every child to show his particular "art work" to the entire class. The opaque projector makes this possible. Such projection enables every member of a large group to see small drawings or objects at the same time. The handiwork of each pupil may be admired and discussed by the entire group. When resources are limited and group participation in the discussion is desired, opaque projecton will enable one to get it.

The opaque projector can be used to present a flat picture filmstrip. Hymns may be projected from a hymnbook and sung by the group. Prayers may be projected from a prayer book and prayed in unison. Financial reports, charts, graphs, small architect's drawings, room arrangement, pictures in books may all be projected at little cost. All one needs is a single clear copy. Everyone can contribute to the visual material. In today's visual-minded world there are illustrations for almost any subject—free for the asking. Objects such as leaves and insects, and materials such as hymnals, picture books, and magazines are projectable.

16. SLIDES

A slide (or transparency) in audio-visuals usually refers to one full frame of 35-mm. film bound in paper or glass sized 2″ x 2″. The aperture, or film portion, 1″ x ¾″, may be vertical or horizontal, depending on which way the camera was held when the picture was taken.

Before the 2″ x 2″ slide became popular the church used a standard stereopticon glass slide 3¼″ x 4″ in size. These slides are still in use, both plain or with frosted glass. Pupils may work with a pencil, crayon, or paint on the frosted glass.

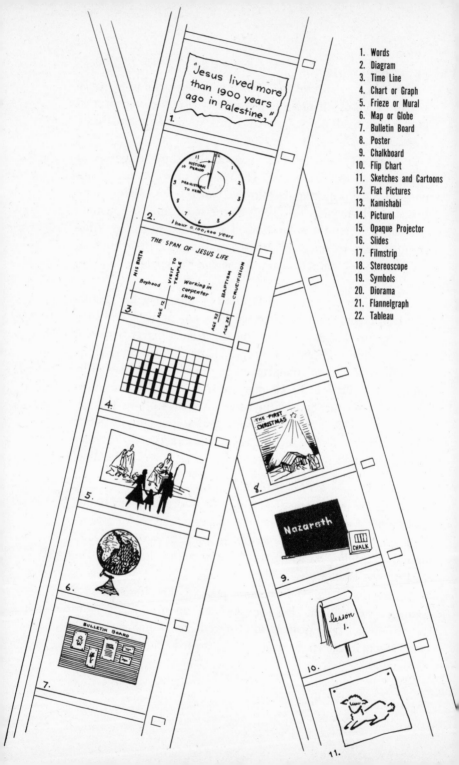

1. Words
2. Diagram
3. Time Line
4. Chart or Graph
5. Frieze or Mural
6. Map or Globe
7. Bulletin Board
8. Poster
9. Chalkboard
10. Flip Chart
11. Sketches and Cartoons
12. Flat Pictures
13. Kamishabi
14. Picturol
15. Opaque Projector
16. Slides
17. Filmstrip
18. Stereoscope
19. Symbols
20. Diorama
21. Flannelgraph
22. Tableau

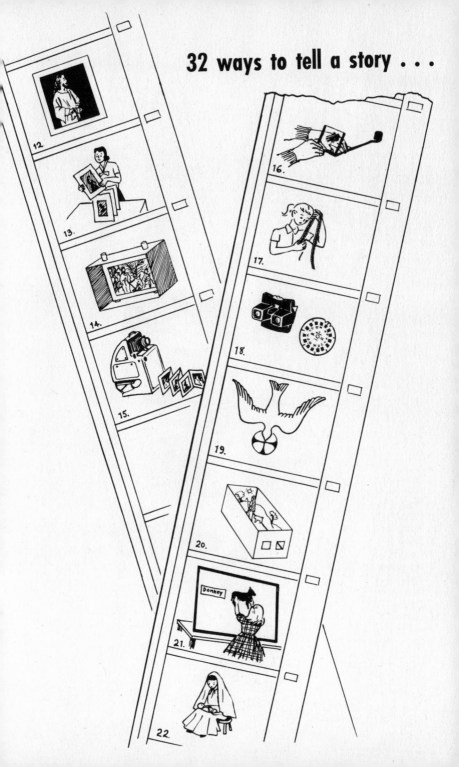

32 ways to tell a story . . .

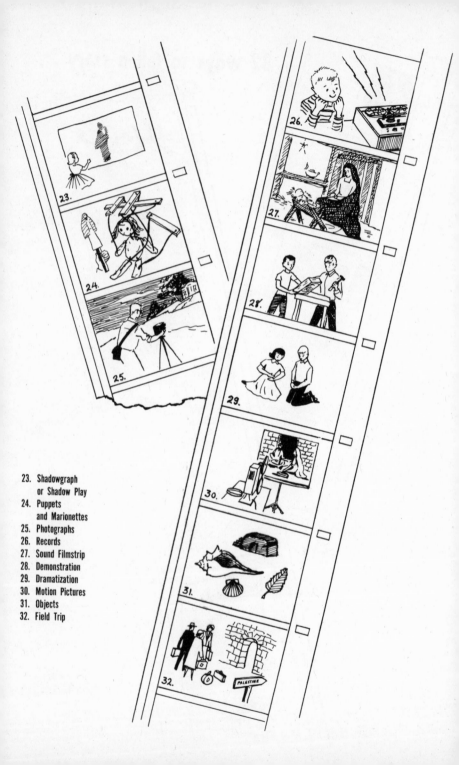

23. Shadowgraph
    or Shadow Play
24. Puppets
    and Marionettes
25. Photographs
26. Records
27. Sound Filmstrip
28. Demonstration
29. Dramatization
30. Motion Pictures
31. Objects
32. Field Trip

A combination slide and filmstrip projector may be used for projecting the 2" x 2" slides. But another projector must be used to project the 3¼" x 4" slides.

Slides made from any good set of pictures of the life of Christ, such as those by Elsie Anna Wood, William Hole, or Jacques Barosin, may be used to tell the story of Jesus. If a committee of children is asked to select the slides and write the story, interest will be heightened. The slides will show persons and settings in a way that will enrich the meaning of the words the children have heard or read.

It is well to bind slides in glass to protect them. One can purchase glass and binders for 2" x 2" slides from a local audio-visual dealer. At this writing S.V.E. (Society for Visual Education) binders are among the best, though new plastic snap-ins are now marketed. Special slide sets such as *Life of Christ* should be protected by binding them in glass. Even the best of projectionists inadvertently gets his fingers on the film portion of an unbound slide. After binding a slide, place it under a heavy object for drying. The heavy object will keep the glass in position and thus make for a well-bound slide. Glass-covered slides may be cleaned with a chamois skin after each use.

The standard stereopticon 3¼" x 4" slides may be bound by laying a piece of glass over the piece of glass on which the visual copy has been produced. If the visual copy is on film, place the film between two pieces of clear glass. Except for permanent use, bind with tabs of adhesive paper. For more permanent use one may write to Keystone View Company, Meadville, Pennsylvania, for information, glass and binding materials, and a free booklet of instructions.

17. FILMSTRIP

A filmstrip is a strip of film 35 millimeters in width containing a series of pictures that tell a visual story. Each picture is called a frame, and filmstrips may have anywhere from a dozen to ten dozen frames, though the average is fifty to sixty each. A filmstrip is projected by a machine known as a filmstrip projector or by a combination slide and filmstrip projector. Most filmstrips are made in color, though some are made in black and white.

A filmstrip like *Palestine in Jesus' Day* will present a story giving background for understanding the life of Christ, showing how Jesus and his family probably lived. A filmstrip allows for a quick change of scenes. There will be less of a break between pictures and, therefore, more of a continuous story. One could use a portion of this filmstrip to create interest in our study.

18. STEREOSCOPE

A stereoscope is a device that enables the viewer to see a still picture in three dimensions. A stereograph (used in the stereoscope) consists of two pictures of the same scene taken from slightly different angles. The pictures are taken with a camera that has two lenses set as far apart as the eyes of a person. The stereoscope enables the two eyes to view the pictures separately but simultaneously. This gives a realistic illusion of three dimensions.

Three-dimensional pictures on a number of biblical subjects, and in various forms, are available to the church school. Though they call for individual use, they add reality to a still picture. They may be placed on the interest or browsing table for the use of those children who arrive early. In the interest of health it is better for each child to have his own stereoscope.

19. SYMBOLS

A symbol is a material object such as a picture, which one can see, representing something abstract, which one cannot see. A manger, a lamb, a scroll, carpenter tools, or a crèche are symbols one could use with junior boys and girls to help them remember the basic elements of this lesson. If one dealt with the last days of Jesus' life, the cross would be an appropriate symbol.

A diorama is a three-dimensional picture seen through an opening. Scenery, properties, and characters are made in miniature. Only the ingenuity of the pupils and the availablity of materials limit the character and uses of the diorama. A diorama may be used to visualize scenes under study. In a peep show they are viewed through two holes in a box, which is lighted from one of the sides or the top.

Several dioramas on this lesson could be made by the children—the manger scene, the carpenter shop, and the dining room of the home of Joseph, Mary, and Jesus. In making a diorama of the dining room some research should be done to discover what Jesus' home may have been like—the nature of the furniture, the color of the walls, the clothes worn, the utensils used, and the food eaten. A simple diorama could be made in this way:

» Use a cardboard box, removing the top and turning it over on its side.

» Draw or paint background scenery on construction paper (or wallpaper or wrapping paper) and paste in the back and sides of the box.

» Make foreground materials of the following:
Papier-mâché—made by
tearing newspaper into bits
pouring boiling water over torn paper
kneading paper into a pulp
removing water
mixing with previously cooked laundry starch to which is added a few drops of oil of cloves
Use papier-mâché to make hills, animals, persons, small properties.
Modeling Clay—purchased at a bookstore or variety store. Use to make small properties, persons, animals.

Salt and Flour Paste—made by mixing two parts of salt to one part of flour and enough water to give it the consistency of paste. Add a few drops of glue. To give the mixture body add some papier-mâché. Use to make animals, persons, small properties, roads, paths, desert. Houses made of salt and flour paste spread over cardboard may be given stone construction effect by pressing rolled oats over the damp surface.

Pipe-stem Cleaners—purchased at a drug store or a variety store. Use to make furniture, people, animals, base for trees, arms for clothespin dolls.

Sponges, pieces of turkish towels—dye green and use to make trees, bushes, and grass; also snip green paper for grass.

Mirrors may be used for lakes; colored paper, for flowers; gray, blue, silver ribbon glued to floor of box will make a winding river.

21. FLANNELGRAPH

Flannelgraph, flannelboard, and feltboard are terms used to describe the materials and the process by which one places a piece of outing flannel on a firm background, set at an angle, and flannel-backed figures and scenes against it to illustrate a story. Flannel sticks to flannel. Before one starts to use it with an audience, explain this fact so the viewing group will not wonder how the teacher performs this amazing feat while they forget to concentrate on what is being audio-visualized.

The flannelgraph has been misused more than any other visual. But it should not be discarded. The real value of this medium lies in having children make and use their own flannelgraph materials. The children should plan and tell the story. They should design, make, and use the materials for illustration. It would be better to draw figures rather than to cut out professionally produced materials.

Using any one of several backgrounds—Nazareth home, manger scene, or carpenter shop—three children could each tell stories of the birth or boyhood of Jesus, illustrating their talks by placing flannel-backed figures against the appropriate backgrounds.

Ask for outing flannel when purchasing flannel at a store or obtaining remnants from homes. Paste or glue may be used to fasten flannel to the backs of figures and properties. The flannelboard should be constructed of a size to suit one's purposes—usually three feet by four feet. Flannel of different colors or dyed flannel will make good background scenes. For example, brown flannel will make mountains; green flannel, grass; and blue flannel, the sky. Or non-colored flannel may be used, on which scenery or properties can be drawn. Unlike a beaded screen that does not produce a good image outside a 45-degree angle from its center, the flannelboard can be seen from almost any angle in a room.

22. TABLEAU

A tableau is a living "still" picture. It is posed by a group of persons so dressed and placed as to represent some historical or fictitious scene.

The use of living still pictures of the several scenes under study would provide participants and viewers with another dimension of learning. Persons could dress as Joseph, Mary, and Jesus, and, using improvised scenery, practice the positions they will take. Actor and viewer will see these scenes long after they have been posed.

23. SHADOWGRAPH OR SHADOW PLAY

A shadowgraph is a picture produced by intercepting light projected against a semitransparent screen such as a sheet, or against a flat white canvas or beaded screen. Children like to intercept light and to form shadows on a screen. They can do this with their hands and fingers or with cutouts of translucent materials such as plastic. Shadows of persons and things may be made on a screen from these cutouts. The nearer one holds the object intercepting the light to the source of the light, the larger the shadow from the object becomes.

By shadow-playing the father-son relationship of Joseph and Jesus in the carpenter shop, one could picture and imitate the conversation one imagines they must have held together. Thus one could help viewers to become acquainted with some of the father-son relationships Joseph and Jesus may have had.

24. PUPPETS AND MARIONETTES

Puppets and marionettes are so much with us on television these days that we can assume general acquaintance with them. Their use on television has promoted use in schools and homes. But the church does not use them enough. Puppets and marionettes enable us to be someone else, to imagine, to dramatize, to state truth vividly, to present information in a very indirect but very palatable form. They caricature. They call forth all the ingenuity and resources we can muster, and they do this at little cost.

Puppets and marionettes are doll-size figures representing persons, things, or animals. Puppets used on a person's hand are called hand puppets. The puppet is moved by the fingers and hand movement of the puppeteer. Other puppets are used on sticks. Puppets on hands or sticks are held above a backdrop, behind which the puppeteer sits or stands.

They may be constructed of many materials. Puppet heads may be made of small boxes, bags, wood, stuffed stocking tops and feet, electric light bulbs, apples, potatoes, rubber balls, or they may be molded from papier-mâché, salt and flour. Puppets may be clothed from remnants of dress goods which the children bring from home.

Marionettes are string-operated from above. Strings are attached to various parts of a marionette's body and fastened to the control, which is made of strips of wood. The strings are

44

manipulated by a person who stands behind and above the stage on which the marionette is made to perform.

Marionettes may be constructed of a greater variety of materials than puppets because it is not necessary to get the forefinger in the head, and two fingers in the arms, for purposes of movement. They may be made of boxes, wood, cardboard, paper rolled and tied together, corn cobs, tubes, or any object that will form the torso of a body. Toys of all types make interesting marionettes. They usually require more skill to produce and operate than puppets. For help in making marionettes consult the book *Marionettes: Easy to Make! Fun to Use!* by Edith Flack Ackley.

Junior boys and girls will delight in making puppets or marionettes of several characters in this study. The experiences they may conjure up as having taken place in the household of Jesus and his parents are almost unlimited. The children will make the figures and the scenery, as well as write and relate the story. In the process the children will learn to think and work together through their actors, as well as live the incidents in the life of Jesus.

25. PHOTOGRAPHS

A photograph (black and white, or color) is a picture produced on a sensitized surface by the chemical action of light. Photographs come in various sizes, as most of us know from having taken pictures ourselves.

Photographs of Palestinian scenes of the birthplace and boyhood environs of Jesus would provide very usable visuals to be carefully observed and studied. In these days of world traveling and much picture-taking, it is more possible to obtain photographs of scenes from the Holy Land. They may be studied and viewed individually or in small groups. They may be placed on the bulletin board or used in an opaque projector. They may be studied in detail.

45

Photographs are much more meaningful when we have taken them ourselves. The class may want to seek out and use the services of amateur or professional photographers in the church. People like to see themselves. They will sharpen up in many ways for a picture of themselves and their group at work. It is important for the church record to have on file photographs taken of all activities and history-making events in the church.

26. RECORDS

A record (transcription) is a recording of sound on disc or cylinder for reproduction by a record player. One may also record on magnetic tape. Records come in varying sizes—from 6 to 16 inches in diameter—the average sizes being 10 and 12 inches. They are recorded and reproduced at one of four speeds —78, 45, 33⅓, or 16⅔ revolutions per minute (rpm). Tape recordings may also be made by the children at either 1⅞, 3¾, 7½, or 15 inches per second, depending upon the type of equipment available.

A mood for this lesson may be created by the use of recorded music such as the Christmas hymns "O Jesus, Once a Nazareth Boy" and "Jesu Bambino" before the class session as part of the worship, or played very softly while the teacher tells portions of the story of Jesus.

Records are inexpensive. They may be used a thousand times. They will last for years. The initial cost is the only concern. Good basic records will be needed for the nursery and kindergarten departments. A record club could be started in the church. Persons may be requested to donate a record selected by a church school department. The donor could be invited to visit the class when it is first used.

The tape recorder is a valuable tool. The initial cost of the machine and tape will be fairly high, but the tape can be used repeatedly. A tape recorder may be used to record scripts, sermons, plays, choir, and meetings. The tape recorder may be used to correct and perfect speech and voice; to take a message to shut-ins; to put on "radio broadcasts" as a program for a group; and to rebroadcast actual radio broadcasts. It would be well if the local church had a "committee on the alert" to take off tapes from radio and television for future use by any interested group.

27. SOUND FILMSTRIP

A sound filmstrip is a filmstrip accompanied by music, narration (or several voices in conversation) and sound effects. Two machines—a record player and a filmstrip projector—are required for the use of a sound filmstrip. If the sound is recorded on tape, a tape recorder is used to reproduce the sound.

The use of a sound·filmstrip like *Holy Child of Bethlehem* (Cathedral Films) will give concreteness to the story of the birth of Jesus. It will provide a realistic setting by which the story will be better remembered. It will present a continuous and well-narrated story or message. This concrete medium of teaching, however, has limitations. It is professionally produced. The record cannot be readily stopped while the group discusses a particular frame in the filmstrip. In using a record for narration, it is difficult to study a filmstrip frame by frame. Better than usual utilization, in terms of introduction and follow-up, is required when using a sound filmstrip. However, a special record player with discussional control is now being marketed which enables the leader to stop the record instantaneously and to start it again without loss of speed, thus reproducing the sound properly.

28. DEMONSTRATION

A demonstration is a description given and explanation made with objects, persons, or specimens in order to establish a truth or make a fact clear.

By the use of a prepared map of Palestine, drawn to a scale of ½ inch to a mile, one could measure the length and breadth

47

and compute the mileage covered in order to travel across Palestine in Jesus' day. It would also be possible to demonstrate a conversation Joseph and Jesus may have held in the carpenter shop, how they may have worked together, making smooth the yokes, or how Joseph, Mary, and Jesus must have talked together about God.

29. DRAMATIZATION

A dramatization is the act of putting a story or an event into some form of drama. Pantomime (silent presentation) is an excellent dramatic medium. Junior children use pantomime well. Role-playing is acting the part of another person in a specific situation.

There are a number of scenes in our lesson that lend themselves to dramatic presentation, such as the journey to Bethlehem, Joseph and Mary looking in the stable, Jesus in the carpenter shop listening to Joseph, or Jesus watching Joseph. Pantomime could show that Joseph taught more by example than by verbal precept, and it is possible to assume this to have been the case. Persons participating in a drama are likely to gain the most from it. A well-presented drama is far more real to juniors than a filmed version (sound motion picture) of the same story.

There is little financial cost involved in role-playing, although if we participate it may cost us some of our false pride. Role-playing brings objectivity to the subject under discussion. One can present a situation where two children find it difficult to share toys. In looking and laughing at the role players, we see ourselves more objectively. Acting out a difference of opinion in a church council meeting or youth meeting will reveal how stubborn and dated some of our positions may be.

30. MOTION PICTURES

A motion picture is a series of single pictures, taken on 8-mm., 16-mm., or 35-mm. film, of certain action cut and arranged in sequence to tell a story or present information. When projected by a motion picture projector onto a screen, these pictures are shown in such rapid succession that they appear to the human eye as actual movement. The split-second change from frame to frame is not detected by the human eye. If the film is sound film, the sounds are recorded on the film alongside the pictures and reproduced in a manner that makes it appear that they are being made at the same moment the persons on the screen are being heard.

For some time it has been possible to record *picture and sound* on tape. When this process is perfected, machines produced in quantity and prices reduced, the church will have to adjust not only to the purchase of new equipment but to this revolutionary teaching medium.

A sound motion picture film like *Child of Bethlehem* (Cathedral Films) or *Childhood of Jesus* (Family Films), when properly previewed, shown, and used will present concretely the major portion of our lesson. A sound film, when well conceived, executed, and used, will give those with whom it is used an almost first-hand experience, and is therefore usually the most concrete audio-visual resource available. The only exception is the actual object or experience. The motion picture can present in an objective manner complex human interaction. The experience level of the viewer should be taken into consideration when using a motion picture or any other audio-visual.

31. OBJECTS

An object or model refers to the thing itself, or a miniature, a mock-up, specimen, or replica of it. A whole series of objects are sometimes collected by a church and exhibited in the local church museum.

One could use a crèche with the figures of Joseph, Mary, and the shepherds adoring the child Jesus in the manger. Junior boys and girls can produce the crèche figures and objects in miniature with modeling clay, papier-mâché, or other material.

They could also make models of a Palestinian home, small scroll, clay lamp, and mezuzah. They will appreciate the contribution of people of Bible times all the more if they read the scroll by the light of their hand-made Bible lamps.

The grade schools in our community have a show time once or twice a week. At such periods any child may show and tell about objects he has brought from home. The objects need not be related to any particular study. It is enough that Ken or Karen are interested in them. The objects are important to them. They have a relationship to their lives and therefore to the lives of their classmates and friends. How many times have children been disregarded when they brought objects to the church school class because the objects "had nothing to do with the lesson"? What is "the lesson" after all? The growing person is our important interest, and his concern is our concern.

32. FIELD TRIP

Taking the church school class or other group to a place where its members are confronted by the real situation which is the subject of study, or a situation closely related to it, may be one of the most effective methods of teaching. We could take a trip to Palestine, although it is not likely that many of us will do so. But if we should happen to journey to Palestine today, we could get some idea of how Jesus, Joseph, and Mary lived and *feel* something of their presence.

Radio and television have been omitted from this listing because there is little likelihood that either could be employed currently for in-class use in connection with the subject under discussion. However, all church leaders should realize more and more how important television and radio are becoming in the lives of our people. It is possible to use certain broadcasts as background information for discussion. Closed-circuit use of television in churches is a possibility in the not too distant future.

No teacher should use more than a few audio-visuals in a single session. Too many resources would get between the teacher and the pupils instead of uniting and assisting them in purposeful activities and experiences.

Our purposes for this chapter have been served, however, if we have demonstrated the almost unlimited possibilities in using audio-visuals to contribute to total learning experience. We will not necessarily need a great deal of money to use audio-visual resources, but we will need all the time, thinking, and ingenuity that teachers and pupils can give.

5

What Works Best with Each Age Group?

❧ ❧ CHILDREN, young people, and adults need to have rich experiences in their church and church school. If the experiences are to be real, they will include some of the following elements. They will appeal to the five senses—sight, sound, smell, touch, and taste. They will be clothed with adventure, newness, and freshness. They will carry a warm, inviting emotional quality. The motivation will be genuine. As is true of all learning, the experience will provide a sense of satisfaction, completion, and synthesis with other experiences. New learning is "built" on old learning, on the known and experienced. Finally, the experiences will involve personal participation, personal satisfaction, and personal achievement.

Every experience of a pupil in the church or church school should involve him in several or all of these elements. The degree to which persons encounter them will determine the richness or poverty of their experience. The learning experiences of persons need to be made memorable, impressive, and varied. We are under obligation to try to make them different as well as real.

Manufactured audio-visuals should be used to add variety and reality to learning. They can be effective supplements to the children's own experiences, but they are by no means to be used as substitutes. They should not replace some more concrete and personal learning experience, nor should they take the place of creative experience or limit the artistic expression of the child. What the child sees can be too readily forgotten. What he experiences is deeply imbedded in his whole being. When children agree to make a series of clay figures of a Palestinian family at home, they express ideas and imaginings concerning that family which are already dormant in their minds, and in so doing they are able to identify themselves more completely with the family.

Most adult leadership in the church has never sought to plumb the depths of children's own audio-visual capacities. Children can not only make their own models from clay but they can also draw their own feelings and conceptions. Children are born artists. They speak, act, mold, and draw out of an inner compulsion. They have already done this inside themselves, and now they bring their imaginings outside in varied forms, not for the world to see but because they must express themselves. When pictures, models, and the words of others are used to teach, the tendency of viewers sometimes is to copy or imitate. To use pictures others have drawn as a means of stretching the imagination of the children in order to inspire them to form pictures in their own minds is the aim of the teacher with a picture collection.

Audio-Visual Materials for Children

Teachers, leaders, supervisors, pastors, superintendents, official board members, and parents will want to bear in mind the special characteristics of children and the children's particular needs and interests as they plan for the use of audio-visuals with them. The way children learn helps to determine what to use and how. Interest time span varies from year to year. In contrast with older children, a child three to six years old responds briefly to almost everything. Direct experience is the most effective way for persons of any age to learn, but children, especially, need direct experience. The children should participate. They are very poor spectators. The sense of feeling is important in the education of younger children. Children should be prepared for what they are to see and hear. Children will, because of their inexperience, need an especially prepared introduction and follow-up of audio-visuals. Older children will want to talk over, discuss, and evaluate what they have seen and heard.

Television has forced us to revise our ideas about the use of projected audio-visuals with children. We now know how their attention and interest are captured by the TV screen. Even young children can and do follow the fast-moving scenes of a film. But we also know that their ability to concentrate, to absorb or understand, and to retain is very limited because they are young and inexperienced.

Hence the audio-visual materials with children should be kept brief. Many pictures divert attention. A few well-chosen slides, or frames of a filmstrip, are better than many pictures. Care in the selection of pictures will enable one to use pictures that focus attention. Fewer details in the pictures and simpler backgrounds make for greater understanding and clarity. The best pictures of Jesus to use with children are those which portray him as warm, friendly, and human. The fifty slides in the Elsie Anna Wood *Life of Christ*[1] series are an excellent resource. Short filmstrips, or longer ones that are designed to be used in units and sections, are the kinds of filmstrips to be purchased by the church school for the children's department.

The nursery, kindergarten, and first-year primary children like

---

[1] Available at your denominational audio-visual library.

NURSERY

to touch, handle, and use things. Objects with which they can do things, preferably large objects, interest them. Flat pictures, simple in detail, are understandable to them, but they prefer to look at their own paintings and those of their friends rather than at pictures which some more experienced artist has executed.

The writer recalls the experience of setting up a sound motion picture projector in the home one evening and projecting a film. His three-year-old son and seven-year-old son had no interest in the pictures being projected on the screen. They stood by the projector, watched the reels turn, saw the lights flicker, and touched the projection table and projector to feel the vibrations. Children like to touch, taste, turn, try, and take. They must be involved.

The way a child handles a flat picture and an object illustrates some of the characteristics of his particular age group. The nursery child accepts a picture of a bird's nest with eggs in it as real. The kindergarten child, who likes to ask questions, will handle an empty bird's nest and compare it roughly with a flat picture of a nest full of eggs or young birds. The primary child will be able to compare details in the bird's nest with the flat picture. The junior child will be concerned with the flat picture, the empty nest, and will go out looking for nests, comparing different kinds of nests. All children will wish to handle the empty bird's nest. Most children, nursery through junior age, will wonder about the empty nest and what happened to the eggs.

The difference between the several age groups may be further illustrated in their use and appreciation of stones. The nursery child will be interested in whether the stones are smooth or rough, light or heavy. As he grows to become a kindergartner he will collect stones, compare colors and textures. The primary child will want to know what kind of stones they are and what they are used for. The junior child will be interested and able to catalog and name them.

The nursery child likes to feel, squeeze, and pat clay. He may make something, but it will be an after-thought. The use of clay will help him channel and use emotional and physical energy constructively. By the use of clay he can express strong feeling without harm to himself or another child. The kindergarten child uses clay for the same reasons. He will make certain crude forms. He will use the clay to express likes and dislikes. The primary child can make readily discernible objects. He can mold recognizable likenesses of persons and things for a diorama that expresses an idea. The junior child can make real likenesses of persons and things. Juniors can project a story with skill. They plan, think, and select on a higher level than primaries. The use of clay is an excellent all-around means of enabling children to express their inner feelings with complete freedom and joyous satisfaction.

Similarly, the nursery child will be interested in a home, his home, but not in looking at or building a Palestinian home. The kindergarten child can appreciate a picture of a Palestinian home. The primary child can make a Palestinian home out of cardboard. The junior child can carve one out of soap.

The nursery child, who lacks complete muscular control, needs large materials with which to work and play. He will work on large sheets of paper, preferably 18″ x 24″ in size, and can make simple markings or strokes with large crayons. He may not be able to keep within the lines of color outline pictures; hence do not use them with him, because they are too exacting, discourage creativity, develop frustrations. The kindergarten child can make drawings of persons and things. He too will need large sheets of paper. He will do free drawings and paintings, spatter painting, finger painting. He will like and learn from large flat pictures. The primary child can plan a specific drawing. He can assume responsibility for making an illustrated book. He can appreciate and help to create and use a mural, frieze, picturol (of his own drawings), dioramas (with paper, clay, or pipe-stem cleaner figures), large-scale models and drawings. He will revel in the use of the opaque projector, for which he may make the visuals. The junior child can make a detailed and skilled painting for a mural or frieze. The pictures will be lifelike and real. None of these age groups needs the guiding hand of a leader to make a perfected product. They need only the freedom and the encouragement that come from appreciative and understanding leaders.

The nursery child lives in a sensory world in the present. He uses toys his small hands can grasp. (But do not give him mechanical toys, because such toys eliminate activity and do not challenge.) He will not appreciate a 2″ x 2″ slide of a toy or a filmstrip depicting children at play. The kindergarten child, who also lives in the immediate moment, will not understand sequence in a filmstrip. Each frame will be just another

picture. He needs to play rather than watch a film of children playing. One may use short filmstrips or a few slides with primary children. Most church motion pictures are beyond them, but they will appreciate and understand the one-reel films that deal with things, people, or actions in keeping with their own experiences. The primary child can project himself outside his immediate environment but he will not understand a time line. The junior child understands sequence and also cause and effect. He will understand a time line. He will not distinguish too well between long-ago times. They are too remote. The long ago of Old Testament and New Testament get all mixed up in his mind.

All ages like to sing. They sing as they work and play. There is a rhythm about their every movement that is natural and expressive. And all ages like to take trips.

Hence the well-planned children's church school rooms will contain the following materials and equipment if they are set up according to age group needs:

Nursery

Browsing center—objects of interest such as growing things, fish, turtles; a magnifying glass; picture books.

Play center—transportation toys, large blocks, balls.

Home center—dishes, stove, etc.

Materials for clay modeling, crayon work, finger and brush painting.

Equipment—flat pictures, slide, frame of filmstrip; stereoscope; piano, record player, and other musical instruments.

KINDERGARTEN

Browsing center—objects of interest such as growing things, fish, turtles; a magnifying glass; picture books.

Play center—transportation toys, large blocks, balls.

Home center—dishes, stove, etc.

Materials for clay modeling, crayon work, finger and brush painting.

Equipment—flat pictures, slide, frame of filmstrip; stereoscope; piano, record player, and other musical instruments.

PRIMARY

Browsing center—objects of interest such as books and growing things.

Materials for clay modeling, mural and frieze, picturol, diorama, painting and drawing, building.

Equipment—bulletin board; flat pictures, large-scale models, a few slides, sections of filmstrips and very short films of activities fitting their age; flannelgraph, opaque projector, stereoscope; piano, record player.

JUNIOR

Browsing center—objects, collections, curios.

Materials for diorama, time line, posters, exhibits, mural and frieze, picturol, sketches, and cartoons.

Equipment—bulletin board, chalkboard, maps, globe; flat pictures, slides, filmstrips, motion pictures; opaque projector, flannelgraph, stereoscope, shadowgraph, puppets, and marionettes; piano, record player, tape recorder.

Often it has been stated that rooms teach. This is particularly true with children. Flat pictures, wall pictures, projected pic-

tures, even teachers need to be at the eye level of the pupils. Objects and materials for interest centers should be at their working level. One should place pictures in appropriate settings. Size of room and size of children are important factors to note. When viewing projected pictures, seat children in straight, narrow rows with a center aisle. It is important to make sure that the children can hear.

All audio-visuals should be integrated into the basic curriculum of the church school. They should be chosen for their value in achieving a particular purpose in the children's work program. We can never emphasize enough the matter of teacher and pupil preparation. Proper preview and planning will help insure wholesome experiences.

It would be well to consult with a denominational or state Christian education department of children's work, and to have a guidance pamphlet on hand, when choosing audio-visual materials. The "Goals for the Christian Education of Children," prepared by the Committee on Children's Work, Division of Christian Education, NCCUSA, should be studied carefully.

With Young People

Using audio-visual materials with young people is even more difficult than with children. Young people are super-critical. They recognize flaws and are critical of productions. They often question the factual basis of conclusions presented. They resist the use of false emotional motivation and of that which their experiences tell them is unreal.

The audio-visuals used with young people should not be out-dated. They should not be up-graded or down-graded. For example, a filmstrip for junior highs on dating should not picture senior highs, and vice versa. If the audio-visual is on a contemporary theme, the costumes should not be of another period of history, and for young people that could mean less than three years ago. If the audio-visual is to deal with personal problems, it too needs to be current.

One cannot interest young people just by announcing that a film or filmstrip will be used next Sunday. They are interested in what is going to be shown. They will want to know if it speaks to their needs, their problems, their wrestlings.

Junior highs are highly emotional, often changing from child to adult and back again. They are active, energetic, and prefer exciting types of materials. They want action. They prefer motion pictures but soon tire of them. Since they can deal with the abstract and can work with ideas and symbols, there is no limit to the variety of audio-visuals usable with them except that the materials need to serve a specific purpose and be well-integrated.

With senior highs[2] one can use most high-quality audio-visuals if they have a part in their selection and use, because they are "almost adults" and want to be treated as such. We need to remind ourselves that audio-visuals are being used with young people in the public schools. Young people may actually be against the use of an audio-visual because of their public school experience. Thus they must have opportunity to have a

---

[2] There is a growing tendency in the church school to divide the six years of junior high-senior high into two-year groupings, instead of the three-year groupings treated here. This would place the 7th-8th graders in junior high, the 9th-10th graders in middle high, and the 11th-12th graders in senior high.

voice in choosing the audio-visuals, just as they help to choose all program elements, and should also be permitted to assist in determining how the audio-visuals are to be used.

With Adults

Our first task in planning for the use of audio-visuals with adults is to learn to know and understand them. In brief, we can say that the older young person is concerned with getting an education, a job, a wife (or husband), a home, and a place in the world. The married young adult wants a better job, a better car, a better home, a child or children, and a more secure place in the world. The middle and older adults tend to seek more of the same. They maintain tradition and resist change. Actually, all of us, from youth to old age, have some of each of these desires. We usually change gradually if at all. We prefer our changes to be imperceptible.

It is generally recognized that certain motivation forces or springs of action cause persons to do the things they do. All healthy persons are motivated by physical need, the urge to grow, the need for security, the desire for affection, the need for recognition and new experiences. Teaching adults should result in changes of behavior, on their part and on the part of the leader. The changes may be in terms of knowledge, skills, attitudes, appreciation, and understanding. We use audio-visual media to create situations, to reinforce and channel ideas so that change can take place. A new type of behavior may then result.

In order that adults may learn and grow, the will to learn and the will to grow must be present. Adults must *want* to learn and *want* to grow. Learning and growing involve them in activity, in participation, and result in continuing satisfactions.

Each adult is an individual. He has his own peculiar experiences that contribute to his uniqueness as a person. Therefore it is wise to plan as well for adults as one does for children and young people.

One should bear these additional principles in mind. We can use audio-visuals with adults, but the audio-visuals chosen should be clear, interesting, and to the point. The adults themselves should select and use the audio-visuals. They are adults and should be treated as such. The audio-visuals should fit the subject matter and serve the purposes for which the adults are gathered together.

Adults are less flexible than children and young people. Patterns of behavior are deep-seated. Adults have done things a certain way longer than young people. In making changes we will proceed with a concern for their years of experience. Adults do not take readily to new methods and procedures. Therefore, it is well to make good, through careful, planning and execution of whatever novel programming one attempts. When confidence is established in leaders and committees, adults of all ages participate quite readily.

Adults, like young people and children, will tire of the use of the same audio-visual medium week after week. Wise leaders will vary both methods and media in working with them.

6

Making the Most of
Flat Pictures

🎵 🎵 FLAT PICTURES belong to all age groups. They may be
used on walls, in worship centers, on bulletin boards, and in
classrooms. They may be used to teach a hymn to children, to
create a setting for worship, for exploration, for questioning.
Flat pictures are available in all sizes. They may be painted,
purchased, or cut out of magazines and collected for future use.

In an era when people are primarily concerned with projected
pictures and three-dimensional pictures, we are in real danger
of overlooking the value of the flat picture. What is more, we
are so surfeited with the use of flat pictures in advertisements
that we are prone to discount their worth in Christian teaching.
What do flat pictures do? What do they mean to children, to
young people, to adults?

Pictures are real for young children. The persons and things
in a picture are real. The time is the present. The action is
taking place here and now. It is a new experience.

For young people and adults pictures are *symbols* of reality.
They remind them of real things. The time is the past. The
action has taken place. When a picture has reality for us, it

means we can translate it into something we have experienced. With experience in our background a picture represents, at least in part, what we understand. Psychologists call this "apperceptive background." Sometimes a picture is misinterpreted—that is, it has been translated into something "understandable" but not at all accurate.

Pictures are used to present information, arouse emotions, and elicit action. We use pictures to cultivate an appreciation of beauty and goodness, to portray persons, places, and events, and to motivate persons to actions like those portrayed in the picture. Pictures may illumine an experience or an idea. They may open a door to new worlds.

Collecting Pictures

Every church school teacher should become a collector of flat pictures. Sizes of pictures, at this stage, are unimportant. There is no limit to the uses one will make of them. The very small pictures may be used in an opaque projector, and they may be handled and viewed individually by pupils. They may also be mounted on mounting paper or board (bristol board is used most frequently) large enough to provide a wide border. Such a border of proportionate width tends to "increase" the size of the picture. The border sets the picture off. It is best to use a neutral shade such as blue or gray.

Pictures should be kept in a metal or wooden dust-proof file. If budget does not allow for the purchase of such a file, obtain a heavy cardboard box. Reinforce it by placing a box within a box or lining the bottom and four sides with another thickness

of cardboard. Insert dividers, clearly labeled, with protruding tabs on which you designate the classification.

All pictures purchased by the church for the use of any given department belong to the whole church. One could make a list of departmental pictures, but keep the pictures in the all-church picture file. It is best to enter the file number after each picture title so you may select and procure the pictures readily when needed.

Teachers will want to collect and file their own pictures for personal use as well as arrange for the adequate filing of church-owned pictures. They will develop a card index of the pictures as they are gathered. Flat pictures, cut out of disposable magazines, should be filed systematically under general headings. Some magazines are too precious intact to be cut up. A separate card file index of their nature and source may facilitate their use.

File pictures according to subject matter. For example, "Animals" could be lettered A, and the several animal pictures filed under the general heading of Animals numbered A-1, A-2, etc. The listing as a whole may include the following:

1. Animals
2. Bible Customs and Places
3. Birds
4. Children
   (a) at play
   (b) at work
   (c) at worship
   (d) of other lands
5. Christmas (The Christ Child)
6. Churches
7. Church Schools
8. Early Christian Church
9. Families
10. Helpers
11. Holy Week and Easter
12. International Missions
13. Jesus as a Boy
14. Jesus Went About Doing Good
15. Jesus Teaching and His Ministry, Stories and Parables Jesus Told
16. Madonnas
17. Maps—Geographical
18. Miscellaneous
19. National Missions
20. Old Testament Heroes
21. Old Testament Stories
22. Summer and Spring
23. Winter and Fall
24. Worship

Additional subdivisions may be used as required.

Pictures are to be marked on the back in the lower right corner. A notebook or card file marked "Section 1. Animals" will contain all the names of the pictures, the names of the artists, and any other information needed to describe the pictures.

Two cross-reference files listing (1) the name of the artist, (2) the title of the picture, would make the above even more helpful. A picture interpretation file arranged by the name of the artist or the title of the picture would add to the usefulness of the pictures.

If the church has been in existence for some time, leaders will want to gather, sort, and file all the flat pictures that have come in the kindergarten, primary, and junior picture sets. These may be stored in a dry place, along with all audio-visual equipment.

It would be well to take a survey of wall picture needs in all

church school rooms. Some pictures will merely need cleaning. Others should be reframed, rehung (at the eye level of the group using the room), and still others should be replaced. A modern church school should purchase at least one new flat wall picture every year.

Wall pictures should be changed from season to season. They should be selected for their specific value to the group in whose room they will be hung. The children, young people, or adults should help in selection and purchase. New pictures will always be forthcoming in supply houses.

The church should be guided by the following principles in the selection and use of pictures. Bear in mind some of the principles presented in chapter 5 regarding what to use with each age group.

Use standard, high quality pictures. The art should have religious meaning and significance. All art selected should be within the range and experience of the persons with whom it is being used. Too frequently, adult standards determine the selection of flat pictures, and the way we were taught determines their use. Most persons are able to appreciate pictures designed for their own age level. They are usually not art critics, nor do they appreciate being harangued with criticism of a flat picture or, for that matter, of a film.

When choosing pictures for children we should ask questions like these: Is the picture within the range of the child's experience? Is the message clear? Will the child take more than a first or second look? Will children honestly *like* the picture?

Which pictures will interest children? Children are interested in children, persons, things, and actions that are a part of their experience. Something pleasant must be happening. They like and understand pictures of their everyday acquaintances and experiences. One may use pictures of nature and of the more familiar New Testament and Old Testament stories.

It is best to avoid the use of pictures portraying children in trouble, doing nothing, or virtually undressed. Confusion reigns for small children when Jesus is pictured as a good shepherd in one picture and a carpenter in another.

Framed pictures for each room have already been mentioned. In addition, one may use pictures for children in picture corners, story illustrations, and to interpret music, visualize Scripture, or provide a setting and point of focus for the worship theme.

Pictures may be overused, overanalyzed, overinterpreted. Beware of picture enthusiasts, just as you guard against an overdose of any good thing. Such enthusiasts may be art failures or successes, but they do as much harm as the person in charge of "flannelgraph education." Certain types of pictures are used because the zealous leader likes them. When the choice is made without relation to the subject matter studied or the interest of others, we violate good teaching practices.

The leader should always use his pictures well. With children, it is best to let the pictures be discovered. One should show the pictures or call attention to them only when necessary. Young people and adults need a chance to let the pictures speak to them. After all, each man's interpretation is, in a sense, the correct one, for he brings to the picture a unique life, a different set of circumstances upon which he has acted. Protestantism has no strait jackets for any of the arts. The discipline of conscience, nurtured in the Christian faith, is guardian and guide enough. The leader may wish later to add meaning to the group's interpretation through a more studied interpretation.

Symbols and symbolic pictures represent things and ideas. They should be reserved for use in later years, after a child has had some experiences with which to interpret them. It is a distinct loss in Christian education that very few churches have any art glass windows intelligible to younger children. And most art glass windows are too small. They remain unseen and unintelligible to the majority of the membership in a congregation. In most instances, the members never had a chance to select the windows. The minister or the official church body did it. What better opportunity for the education of the total church than through participation in this important matter of window selection!

Sources

Pictures may be purchased from any denomination resource center, audio-visual agency, bookstore, or supply house. They will handle most of the subjects of the following picture houses:

New York Graphic Society
10 West 33rd Street
New York 1, New York

Art-Lore, Inc.
15 West 28th Street
New York 1, New York

Society for Promoting Christian
  Knowledge
Northumberland Avenue
London, W. C. 2, England

Artext Prints, Inc.
Westport, Connecticut

Erich S. Herrmann, Inc.
225 Fifth Avenue
New York 10, New York

The Colonial Art Company
1336-1338 N. West First Street
Oklahoma City 4, Oklahoma

International Art Publishing
  Co., Inc.
243 West Congress Street
Detroit 26, Michigan

The Perry Pictures Company
Malden, Massachusetts

University Prints
11 Boyd Street
Newton, Massachusetts

National Gallery of Art
Washington 25, D. C.

Consult also the art institute nearest you.

Pictures worthy of a place in the minds and hearts of people

are deserving of a place on the walls of church school rooms.
Such are the following.

NURSERY

Correggio	Holy Night
Ferruzzi	Madonna of the Streets
Plockhörst	Jesus Blessing the Children
Raphael	Sistine Madonna
Tarrant	Morning Carol
	The Lesser Brethren
Vichon	Christ with Children
Wood	Jesus and the Children

KINDERGARTEN

Ferruzzi	Madonna of the Streets
Plockhörst	Jesus Blessing the Children
Raphael	Sistine Madonna
Smith	We Give Thee Thanks
Soord	The Lost Sheep
Tarrant	All Things Wise and Wonderful
	Morning Carol
	The First Flower Service
	Suffer Little Children
	The Lesser Brethren
	The Star of Bethlehem
Vichon	Christ with Children
Wood	Jesus and the Children
	No Room at the Inn
	Of Such Is the Kingdom of Heaven

PRIMARY

Briggs	Jesus in the Workshop
Copping	The Hope of the World
	Jesus and the Newsboys

71

Correggio	Holy Night
Curr	Follow Me
L'Hermitte	Among the Lowly
Plockhörst	Jesus Blessing the Children
Raphael	Sistine Madonna
Reynolds	Infant Samuel at Prayer
Smith	We Give Thee Thanks
Soord	The Lost Sheep
Tarrant	All Things Wise and Wonderful
	He Prayeth Best Who Loveth Best
	Morning Carol
	No Room at the Inn
	Suffer Little Children
	The Lesser Brethren
	The Star of Bethlehem
Wood	Jesus and the Children
	Jesus Teaching from a Boat
	The Call of the First Disciples
	The Good Samaritan
	The Friend
	The Teacher
Zimmermann	Christ and the Fishermen

JUNIOR

Barosin	The Carpenter Shop
Copping	The Hope of the World
	Jesus and the Newsboys
Curr	Follow Me
Hofmann	Christ at Twelve
	Christ at Thirty-three
	Christ in the Temple
L'Hermitte	Among the Lowly
Soord	The Lost Sheep

Tarrant	Behold I Send You Forth
	He Prayeth Best Who Loveth Best
	No Room at the Inn
Wood	Jesus Teaching from a Boat
	The Call of the First Disciples
	The Good Samaritan
	The Friend
	The Teacher
	The Hilltop at Nazareth

JUNIOR AND SENIOR HIGH

Borthwick	The Presence
Da Vinci	The Last Supper
Hardy	Worship of the Nations
Hunt	The Light of the World
Larson	Thy Kingdom Come
Munkascy	Christ Before Pilate
	The Crucifixion
Rosenkrantz	The Omnipresent
Soord	The Lost Sheep
Todd	The Nazarene
Wood	The Sermon on the Mount
	The Hilltop at Nazareth

OLDER YOUNG PEOPLE AND ADULTS

Barosin	The Great Commission
Borthwick	The Presence
Burnand	Go Preach
Da Vinci	The Last Supper
Fügel	The Last Supper
Hole	If Thou Hadst Known, Oh Jerusalem
Millet	The Gleaners
	The Man with the Hoe
	The Angelus
	La Bergere

Munkascy	Christ Before Pilate
	The Crucifixion
Rosenkrantz	The Omnipresent
Soord	The Lost Sheep
Todd	The Nazarene
Wood	The Feet Washing
	The Cleansing of the Temple
	The Resurrection

A balance should be kept in the pictures one places in any room. Adults should have pictures ranging from the birth through the resurrection of Jesus. These should never be limited to one or two artists or one particular period in history or one nationality. The church should use the early Italian, the 14th-century German, the 19th-century French, the 20th-century American, or some other similar choices. It would be good to obtain Oriental prints of some of these subjects. Jesus Christ belongs to all his followers. If a German artist or Italian artist sees something of the German or Italian in Jesus, so does the Oriental see in him something of the Japanese or Chinese. If Jesus belongs to the Orientals, he should be seen as they see him. To see Jesus Christ only as one artist portrays him is limiting. To see him as several artists conceive him helps enlarge our conception of him. He is more than any one of us can think or paint.

7

Before and After
Projecting Audio-Visuals

𝕏 𝕏 CERTAIN BASIC STEPS are essential to good utilization. The leader and his assistants, whether children, young people, or adults, need to adopt and follow these steps carefully:

The leader should know the group—their experience, knowledge, and skills.

He should know the lesson material or subject matter to be taught.

Then he should select the media of imparting the knowledge, motivating the group, or teaching the skill.

The printed materials should be previewed. If the audiovisuals are available, they too should be previewed.

As far as possible one should go to the session completely prepared. Part of the preparation will be the development of the ability to adjust and vary one's plans and procedures to meet the developing needs of the group. For example, one might plan to show a film only once, but the discussion and resulting differences in interpretation of facts might call for a second showing immediately or at a later session. Or one might have planned for the reading of the script of a filmstrip in its entirety, but a

member of the group raises a question. Stopping to answer or discuss the question could be of more value than finishing the reading of the script at that time.

Prepare the Group

Each person comes to a given session out of a different background. Each person has a number of special interests and problems, goals, and achievements. One cannot assume that a certain number of persons called a group, or organization, or fellowship are together in their thinking. They may be merely an aggregate of individuals waiting for proof of the leader's ability to hold their interest, some even defying him to get them off their trolley and on his train, or better still the group's train. Members of a class or group may not be with the group in thinking at that moment when a committee, or even a leader, throws a film or filmstrip on the screen. Even the introductory part of a film may not necessarily get everyone thinking together. Like horses at a race, members of a group must be brought up to the starting line by the leader if all members are to get an equal start.

What is one's purpose in projecting an audio-visual? There must be a well-established reason for using it, and that reason should be made clear to the group. Edgar Dale of Ohio State University has coined the word *coik*, which applies to all ways of learning. It means "clear only if known." The purpose should be clear and made known before an audio-visual is projected. New learning takes place on old learning; thus it is well to build on previous knowledge. The audio-visual, the subject under discussion, the group, and one's purposes in showing the audio-visual need to be taken into consideration as it is introduced. These are some questions the users of audio-visuals may want to ask and answer:

» What do we want the group to look for in the audio-visual?
» What do we want them to learn?
» How do we want them to feel?
» What do we want them to do?
» Are there any known prejudices?
» Is anyone misinformed?
» What changes in thinking may we expect them to make?
» How will we follow up after the showing?

In planning utilization, keep certain fundamental principles in mind. One must stick to the purposes but not violate the needs of individual persons (such as answering their questions) in order to conform to some previously established system of using an audio-visual. It ought to be possible for members of the group to present, show, and follow up the use of the audio-visual. Sharing responsibility is basic Christian stewardship. The leader should never do for the group what members of that group can do for themselves. Ministers have enough to do. It would be better to arrange for lay people, lay ministers, members of the group to operate equipment and assist in the guiding and teaching program.

Select Readers

Many reading filmstrips are available to churches. They deal with many subjects and are the stories of persons of various ages. The filmstrip settings are in different lands and about different people. In selecting readers it would be well to do so in keeping with the age and sex of the filmstrip narrator. The spirit in which the story is told should be borne in mind. The great variety of voices of young and old available in the church should be used. They should be chosen as one would select actors for a play. No one person should narrate or record all the scripts. This applies to the pastor, the director of religious education, and that special baritone who has been assigned more work than any church member should be asked to do.

How to Introduce

The introduction should be brief and to the point, because it can bore an audience into disinterest even before they see a film. The leader will try not to leave them in the dark as to his purpose. If necessary, the basic purpose may be stated twice, plus having it written on a chalkboard or chart. The interest of the group should be captured, and their imagination should be excited. Beware, however, of the spectacular and the flamboyant. It is advisable not to amaze for sheer amazement's sake, for that only leads to confusion and frustration.

Sameness in anything can be deadening, and introductions to audio-visuals are no exception. Since not all projected audio-visual subjects are the same, the introductions should be varied also.

There are a number of ways to help persons get at the inherent content of an audio-visual. The leader may present the thread of the story. He may refer to the persons in the presentation, the places where the events occurred, or the events themselves. He may ask the group to look for answers, questions, solutions, relationships, comparisons, or facts.

New ways of introducing audio-visuals will heighten interest and lead to greater learning. Good teachers and leaders will use their own best gifts in this teaching enterprise. One could use introductions like the following:

(1) A written statement on what to look for in the audio-visual may be read. The list should be kept short, preferably as one general statement; such as, "Remember the names of all persons mentioned in this filmstrip"; or, "What decisions did

people make in this film?" If users will look for and remember names of persons and their decisions, they will recall much of what is related to each.

(2) The question-and-answer method of introducing an audio-visual stimulates interest. Two persons up front, one on each side of the room, may ask and answer several questions that will direct the attention of the viewers to several important elements in the audio-visual for which the group should be looking.

(3) Sometimes a few well-chosen questions will suffice to heighten interest and get the attention of the group.

(4) A portion of the story to be presented in a film may be dramatized. A person dressed somewhat as the chief character may be asked to depict the basic conflict or change by stating certain key sentences the group is to look for and remember. It is also possible to use a dialogue sequence or role-playing for this purpose.

(5) If the audio-visual is devotional in character, there could be no better introduction than a service of worship. The service should be arranged in such a way that it introduces and is in keeping with the audio-visual used. If one introduces the audio-visual in a devotional mood, it is good to close in a devotional mood. Hymns, scripture, and prayers should be in keeping with the theme of the audio-visual.

(6) For a filmstrip on the life of some biblical personality, the leader may read a passage of Scripture that introduces his story or that summarizes his basic contribution as visualized. A film on the story of Zacchaeus could be introduced by reading Luke 19:1-10. A film on a parable of Jesus would call for a reading of the parable itself and possibly a rereading emphasizing the key sentences.

(7) Stating or reading the key sentence in a film or filmstrip will alert the viewing group and cause them to look for it throughout the showing period.

(8) Listing the basic points presented in an audio-visual, and reading them to the group before use, is another way of introduction. One could use a filmstrip like *The Growth in Our Idea of God*[1] in this way by stating directly from the script a half-dozen beliefs about God that people held in Bible times. Then the filmstrip could be shown.

(9) Members of the group may be asked to state, or write on paper, their own ideas of a subject, preceding the showing of the audio-visual. By group participation one could then correct any misconceptions or fill in where there is still lack of knowledge.

(10) Two sheets of a turn-over chart can be used to help introduce and utilize an audio-visual. On the right half of the second sheet list the several points made in the filmstrip. Cover with the first sheet. Split the first sheet in the center vertically, and on the left half record the class's ideas concerning the subject that is to be presented. Then show the filmstrip. After the showing turn over the blank right half of the first chart sheet so that the group can see their ideas in contrast to the ideas previously recorded directly from the filmstrip script.

Follow-Up

The follow-up in the use of an audio-visual should have a direct relationship to the introduction. If a question is asked in the introduction, it should be dealt with in closing. If one begins with a scripture reading, it would be well to close with the same or another reading. If a worship setting and mood were established in the introduction, the follow-up should be done in that same manner and spirit. If the rather self-contained audio-visual is worshipful in mood and draws its own conclusion, the close may be a simple prayer or a benediction.

---

[1] Produced by the Evangelical and Reformed Church and Congregational Christian Churches.

Once a purpose is stated to the group, one has in most instances determined the follow-up procedure. Presenting some facts through the use of an audio-visual will call for a review of those facts to see that they have been learned. The review may include a test and possibly a reshowing of the audio-visual.

The use of the audio-visual should be timed so there will be an unhurried follow-up. As in the case of the introduction, so with the follow-up, it is good to be brief. The obvious should not be labored. The intelligence of the audience should not be insulted by telling them what they have seen. If they wish to recall the contents of the audio-visual, it may be to their advantage to do so.

Of course, the follow-up may vary from the introduction if the group needs, evidenced in the process of use, indicate that variation from the original plan is desirable.

Some General Principles of Utilization

Sufficient experimentation and research by colleges and universities, the army and navy, the public schools, and the church have been carried on for us to set down some general principles of utilization. As the leader uses projected audio-visuals, he will want to bear them in mind and apply them.

The most direct experience involving the greatest participation usually makes for the best learning situation.

Participation on the part of the viewers contributes to interest, learning, and remembering.

Preparation of the group for the use of an audio-visual heightens interest, focuses attention, clarifies the purpose, and increases learning.

Stopping a film or filmstrip for purposes of discussion, clarification, or the asking and answering of questions enhances use, but must be done with care and in the best interest of the group.

Answers to questions raised about an audio-visual, given immediately before or after the showing, will increase learning.

Group discussion of a subject is a better type of introduction than one presented by the leader alone. This also applies to follow-up.

A second showing increases learning. Seeing an audio-visual, especially a fast-moving film, at least twice increases the total amount learned.

Use of a film, filmstrip, and chart as a unit with a group is commonly called a packaged approach. Such a package should have unity and build to a common purpose.

Knowledge of the results of the accuracy of one's response, commonly known as "feedback," increases learning. A combination test and review makes for more effective use of an audio-visual.

Practice of a skill, a method, or an ideal presented in an audio-visual helps insure learning.

Seeing, hearing, speaking, and writing foreign or other unknown words quickens learning and increases retention. Flashcards, a chalkboard, and a tape recorder may be used for this purpose.

Using the Filmstrip *Life of Paul*[2]

Let us assume that one is using the *Life of Paul* filmstrip with a group of senior high young people in their course of study on

---

[2] Produced by the Evangelical and Reformed Church and Congregational Christian Churches.

the great apostle to acquaint the class with the basic facts regarding Paul's life, the persons who affected his life, the places in which he lived and worked, and the events that helped to shape his life. Early in the course, as an introduction to it, a committee could plan for the showing of the filmstrip.

The committee could be asked to make a list of the persons, places, and events presented in the filmstrip from the script for adults. They might want to put down in chronological order the names of persons, the events in which they were involved, and the places where the events occurred, as follows:

Persons	Events	Places
Saul	Birth	Tarsus
Parents	Named son after King Saul	
Father	Saul inherited Roman citizenship from him	
Saul	Tent-maker	
Gamaliel	Saul studied under him	Jerusalem
"Christ-followers"	Saul encountered them	
Stephen	Saul present at stoning of him	
"Christ-followers"	Crusade against them	
"Christ-followers"	Fled persecution	Jerusalem and beyond
Saul and "Christ"	Saul's conversion	On road to Damascus
Saul	Baptism	Damascus
Saul	Spiritual struggle	Arabia
Jews	Saul's success as evangelist and danger from Jews	Damascus
Friends	Saul's escape in basket	
Christians	Saul suspected by Christians	Jerusalem
Barnabas and Peter	Saul arrested as "Follower of the Way"	
Barnabas	Christianity attracting non-Jews	Antioch
Saul and Barnabas	Followers first called "Christians"	

The above list covers only 22 frames of the filmstrip, but that is sufficient for purposes of illustration.

Before projecting the pictures and reading the script, divide the class into three equal groups, asking the first group to concentrate on remembering persons; the second, events; and the third, places. After seeing the filmstrip, make three parallel lists on chart paper from the suggestions of the group. Then proceed by asking for an early event or a place or a person mentioned in the filmstrip. Do not allow a class member to answer outside his group responsibility, or to answer a second time until other members have had a chance or until no one else in the group volunteers. After obtaining an answer under one of the headings, such as "event," ask a member in each of the two remaining groups to indicate the place where it happened and to whom it happened. The leader and the committee will have the list before them and will know the filmstrip well enough so the answers may be elicited in the chronological order in which they are believed to have occurred.

It would be good teaching to see the filmstrip again to fill in the remainder of the items which the group may not have recalled. For this purpose the leader may wish to pause at the end of one or more frames, allowing, at this point, anyone in the class to suggest answers.

The charts of parallel listings may be kept for future reference. As one proceeds with the study of the apostle, additional items may be added. A map of the eastern Mediterranean world of Paul's time would help to locate events.

A time line may also be used, showing the time relationship to the life of Jesus and the writing of the Epistles and the Gospels. A time line could be placed vertically on the chart if space permitted.

As the teacher or leader proceeds, the use of additional audiovisuals will suggest themselves.

Using the Filmstrip Amos[3] with Juniors

The filmstrip *Amos* was used with a group of ten junior children in a manner that we believe suggests a variety of values and uses for this and other filmstrips. The boys and girls had been studying about the prophets. It was suggested that Amos was one of the most interesting of the Old Testament prophets. The class agreed to look up information on Amos. The teacher agreed to find out about slides or filmstrips and, if possible, obtain a filmstrip on the life of this prophet.

Prior to the Sunday church school session when Amos was used, a committee of juniors and the teacher reviewed the filmstrip and planned for its use at the end of the following worship service:

PRELUDE

CALL TO WORSHIP

Let us worship the Lord with songs and prayers. Let us think about kindness and goodness, about love and justice.

HYMN: "I Would Be True"

PRAYER: Selected stanzas of the hymn "Take My Life, and Let It Be," read alternately as a prayer by two committee members.

HYMN: "Lord, I Want to Be a Christian"

OFFERING: Use the music of the previous hymn by continuing to play softly while the leader says:

Thy work, O God, needs many hands
　To help thee everywhere,
And some there are who cannot serve
　Unless our gifts we share.

RESPONSE: "We Give Thee But Thine Own"

[3] Produced by Bureau of Audio-Visual Aids, Evangelical and Reformed Church.

85

HYMN: "Dare to Be Brave"

SCRIPTURE: Amos 1:1; 5:14-15, 23-24

INTRODUCTION and USE OF THE FILMSTRIP

The committee had agreed to have the teacher introduce the prophet Amos, the book and its message. The teacher placed difficult words and new names on the chalkboard so the children would understand them when read from the Bible or the filmstrip script. Using the scripture references the children looked up the answers to these questions and answered them in the order given:

(1) Find the Book of Amos in your Bible.

(2) What do we call a person like Amos? Amos 7:14-15

(3) What did Amos do before he became a prophet? Amos 1:1

(4) In what country did he live? Amos 1:1

(5) Where did he preach? Amos 3:1

(6) What special verse of scripture do we remember Amos by? Amos 5:24

(7) Amos had some dreams. What were they about?
Amos 7:1 (locusts)   Amos 8:1 (basket of fruit)
Amos 7:4 (fire)   Amos 9:1 (Lord by altar)
Amos 7:7 (plumb line)

(8) King Jeroboam II had a special prophet who usually agreed with him. What was that prophet's name? Amos 7:10

(9) Why was Amos concerned? Because he felt God was concerned? See Amos 8:4 ff. Amos told the people they had done wrong. Amos 1:6, 11

(10) Map study: Darken the room and project frame 9 of the filmstrip. Ask the children to name the countries surrounding Israel.

86

The teacher then placed her hand over the lens of the film-strip projector and turned back to frame 4. The script for children was read by one of the committee members, who had prepared himself to do so.

Upon completion of the filmstrip the class reviewed the pictures and told the story of Amos in their own words. They closed their session by saying together the words of Amos 5:24.

USING A FILMSTRIP ON MISSIONS WITH JUNIORS

Ten boys and girls planned for a church school session of one and a half hours on the theme "All Men Are Brothers." Each class member agreed to gather some pictures, from current magazines and newspapers, of boys and girls from other lands. The children were asked to bring objects from foreign lands to the class. They were to obtain these curios, gifts, and mementos from their homes. One boy made a large sign about the theme and placed it on the class bulletin board. In addition, the teacher suggested the use of the filmstrip *Anil of Tilda*.[4]

The class was divided into four committees to plan for the bulletin board, curio table, pictures, and the use of the filmstrip.

The session began with the arrival of the first child, when the teacher examined his pictures and "objects" of interest from other lands. As others came, more pictures were added to the

---

[4] Produced by the Bureau of Audio-Visual Aids, Evangelical and Reformed Church.

bulletin board, and more objects placed on the table. Each child later had a chance to show the things he had brought from another land and to tell about them. The class talked about the people who made them, where the people lived, and some of the things they did. They discussed the likenesses among all boys and girls, and some of the differences, and listed them on the chalkboard. They tried on a sari, jewelry, and headgear like what the people of India wear. The children who wore them kept them on as the filmstrip was shown.

Two juniors, a boy and a girl, had previewed the filmstrip *Anil of Tilda* with the teacher. The teacher suggested that the children turn their chairs so they could see the screen. The girl projected the pictures as the boy read the script. *Anil of Tilda* is the story of a boy of India, his two sisters, and his parents. Anil is shown at work and play, in school and church, and in trouble. The next to the last frame is a scene showing the family seated on the ground having family devotions. This was left on the screen.

The leader and her committee of two suggested a dramatization of this scene. They selected a father, mother, two sisters, and Anil, and seated them in the proper positions. Of course, the girl wearing the sari became the mother. The father was given the Bible and read from Matthew 7:12. Anil prayed the prayer. They all sang. The projector light was turned off, and the class session was completed.

The audio-visuals used were: flat pictures, objects, bulletin board, chalkboard, filmstrip, and drama. The filmstrip was integrated with a total teaching plan. It was only one of several audio-visuals. The junior boys and girls remained central in the teaching situation. Their growth and understanding increased, for among their friends they numbered boys and girls from around the world, and especially an Indian boy named Anil.

8 |

How to Organize for Audio-Visuals

✻ ✻ TEACHERS, program leaders, and persons with audio-visual responsibility are part of a team even in the smallest of churches. Their work is interdependent. They cannot properly and adequately work alone. All leaders in the church have a basic responsibility to assist in organizing for the local church use of audio-visuals.

No two local churches stand at exactly the same point in their use or non-use of audio-visual materials. Each church will need to begin where it is. Every church has a program. Every church has audio-visual materials. So begin!

Audio-visual materials belong to the whole church. No one organization has a monopoly on materials, methods, competence, equipment, or needs. Therefore it is essential to have coordination throughout the whole church organization. Each local church of the various Protestant denominations is structured somewhat differently. But all denominations have a consistory, church council, or church board of some kind that is responsible for the total local church operation and amenable to the congregation.

Set Up an Audio-Visual Committee

In keeping with the organization, structure, and constitution of your church, and in the interest of every phase of its work, the local church should set up an audio-visual committee with a chairman (coordinator), librarian, assistant librarian, and such other persons as are deemed necessary to the best functioning of the committee. The committee will be a part of the over-all program planning body of the church.

It is advisable to have a strong working committee, even in a small church, though care should be exercised to avoid setting up more organization than is needed. The committee should be organized to expedite procurement, storage, and the full use of audio-visuals by all groups in the church.

The committee should be completely representative. Its membership should come from all departments of the church school and all organizations of the church. All ages should be represented. Young people should be on the committee. The committee should include a member of the consistory, or church council, and be amenable to the official body of the church. The committee should not be weighted with mechanics, amateur photographers, or gadgeteers. Some persons with special interests, ability, and skill will be needed, but these persons need not all be placed on the committee.

Creative teaching and good learning experiences call for full participation by the pupils, who should do many things in the audio-visual field themselves. However, there are a number of contributions to teaching and programming that would better be made by persons with special skills. Without taking away responsibility from individual members in the class or group with which one is working, it is possible to use the services of persons like the following:

secretary—to keep records, send notices, post information

writers—to make charts, write on chalkboards or newsprint charts

artists—to draw sample pictures and posters, guide pupils, arrange bulletin board displays, and assist in directing painting (finger painting, spatter printing, water coloring)

persons—to work with their hands, using clay or papier-mâché

persons—to construct with wood, paper, or other materials

dramatists—to direct role-playing, dramas, skits, pageants, and pantomimes

mechanics—to be in charge of storage, maintenance, and the use of equipment, with enough assistants from various organizations (including the women) to operate equipment

at any meeting any time of the day or evening. Only experienced operators should handle the more intricate equipment.

A committee will want to work out its own way of discovering the abilities and skills of all church members. Usually the church obtains such information when persons join the church or during the annual Every Member Canvass. In a day when so many couples, and more specifically parents, are teaching together in the church school, it is time-saving to be able to call for the assistance of persons with special skills.

A person with a fairly complete knowledge of the ongoing program of the church, and the educational program and curriculum of the church school, should be on the committee as coordinator. He and his assistants (committee members) should be in a position to offer suggestions and counsel regarding the use of audio-visuals.

It is desirable that the audio-visual coordinator (chairman of the audio-visual committee) be a member of the local church committee on Christian education. Such an appointment should be made, however, on the basis of competency rather than official relationship. The coordinator will participate in the meetings of the committee on Christian education, as well as the meetings of the various organizations of the church. Thus he, and members of his committee, will be informed regarding future plans and activities of the whole church and be able to give "on the spot" guidance, direction, and advice.

We would logically assume that such a coordinator might, in the normal course of events, develop sufficient competency to train others in the use of audio-visuals. If not, he would at least help plan for and set up training opportunities that are directly related to the leadership program of the church.

One of the coordinator's functions would be to participate in the extended annual meeting prior to the local church and church school "year," with persons holding leadership and teaching responsibilities present from all areas of the church's life. In some churches this takes the form of a retreat to plan the year's work. At this meeting the coordinator would provide an up-to-date listing of audio-visuals available in the local church, announce the titles of new audio-visuals pertinent to the work planned, and give instructions regarding changes in the operation of the audio-visual library. With program plans fairly well organized and outlined, tentative plans would be made for using as many varied audio-visuals as were considered necessary and advisable.

Under no circumstances should committee members determine the program content of any group or class. The committee members and the coordinator act in the capacity of assistants and counselors. They advise, guide, and assist in the use of audio-visuals related to a program previously determined by the group, class, department, or organization asking for the service of a committee member.

The committee will meet periodically, as need requires, always arranging for meeting dates in advance, and they will not meet unless it is necessary. When they meet, the time should be used advantageously. For example, the teachers and department leaders should meet prior to each quarter of the church school year, with the audio-visual coordinator (chairman) and their own representative on the committee present, to preview, evaluate, and arrange to purchase, make, or obtain audio-visual materials to be used. In case an audio-visual comes with the curriculum material, the audio-visual committee representative will assist in scheduling its use in the interest of the total church school.

The Librarian

The librarian (in smaller churches librarian and coordinator may be one and the same person), with an assistant, if needed, will schedule equipment and book materials for use. He (or she) will notify the church office to order all authorized "purchase and rental materials" requested, give general notice to all committee members and organizations of what has been ordered and for what date. (The coordinator or librarian might conceivably suggest a second or even a third use of a film rental for a given Sunday.) The librarian will keep records, checking materials and equipment out and in. He will route the use of machines, like filmstrip projectors, record players, and tape recorders, if two groups plan to share an instrument on a given Sunday morning.

The librarian or an assistant (a committee member) will need to file and have readily accessible all audio-visual materials like filmstrips and scripts, sound filmstrips, flat pictures, slides, maps, posters, cutouts, magnetic tape, and records. He will develop, or have made, a local church catalog of all church-owned audio-visuals and give the catalog to any leader for use in programming.

The librarian will have charge of all church-owned audio-visuals. For example, flat pictures and maps have usually been kept somewhere in the department originally ordering them. The time has come to re-examine this procedure. From the experience of a good many churches, a central depository or library in the local church for all basic audio-visual materials and resources is believed to be preferable. Some logical system must be developed for cataloging, filing, finding, and booking materials for use.

One audio-visual counselor's manual[1] suggests that an A.V. bulletin board be used to list materials ordered, newly purchased, or available if ordered. Sections of the bulletin board could be marked off for the use of each department and organi-

---

[1] *Manual for Training the Audio-Visual Counselor.* Office of Audio-Visual Education, Board of Christian Education, Presbyterian Church, U.S.A.

zation of the church. A bulletin board smartly designed and frequently updated would promote the use of audio-visuals. It would be an easy means of communicating with the users as well as those with whom the material is to be used. The teacher or person wishing an audio-visual for use in his class or organization would consult his local church audio-visual listing of materials. If necessary, he would seek the assistance of the audio-visual librarian and look at the available film guides. He would place his order on some such form as the following and give it to the librarian:

ORDER FOR AUDIO-VISUALS

Title of the audio-visual _____ Date _____

Second choice _____ Date _____

Producer[2] _____

Film ___ Sound filmstrip ___ Filmstrip ___ Records ___ Slides ___

Other _____

Date of use _____ Date needed for preview _____

Place to be used _____ Group _____

Name of person ordering _____ Charge to _____

In our library _____ Rental _____ Purchase _____

The librarian will use a confirmation form in triplicate something like the following. One copy of the form is for the user, one for the church secretary, one for the audio-visual file.

_____

[2] Give the full name of the producer. Today there are a number of duplicate titles. The one distinguishing feature about your order may be the name of the producer.

COPY OF USER'S ORDER

Title of audio-visual _____ Date _____

Second choice _____ Date _____

Producer _____

Film ___ Sound filmstrip ___ Filmstrip ___ Records ___ Slides ___

Other _____

Date of use _____ Date needed for preview _____

Place to be used _____ Group _____

Name of person ordering _____ A. V. Secretary _____

Bill to be paid by _____

In our library _____ Rental _____ Purchase _____

By this means he will notify the user that the order has been placed, notify the secretary of the church to order same, and have a third copy of the order on file. The user's copy may be placed in the department mailbox, or on the bulletin board in the area designating his or her department or organization, or given personally.

When the confirmation of booking comes from a film agency it will be filed and notice will be given on the bulletin board that the film ordered will be available on the date requested. One may prefer to give notice in person or by telephone.

When a film has been booked, ordered, and confirmed, the assignment of a projectionist is in order. It is better to have a projectionist from the group (junior high up) to operate the equipment. Simpler equipment may be operated by older primaries and juniors. It is advisable to supervise those who are just beginning. Some form should be developed by which the projectionist obtains complete instructions. The form should include as a minimum the following:

PROJECTIONIST'S WORK SHEET

Projectionist's name _____

Date to project _____

Time _____ Room _____

Teacher _____ Group _____

Assistant projectionist _____

EQUIPMENT NEEDED

Check items needed: Title of A-V _____

Motion picture projector _____

Filmstrip projector _____ Slide attachment _____

Cart _____ Stand _____ Screen _____

Tape recorder —— Tape —— Record Player —— Speed ——

Short extension cord _____ Long extension cord _____

INSTRUCTIONS

(Equipment should aways be examined and tested before it is put away. This does not provide sufficient insurance, however; so follow through on these suggestions.)

Set up projector _____ Check sound _____

Check projector lamp _____ Project _____ Rewind _____

Injury to the film? _____ Clean gate, lens, and glass _____

Pack equipment as received _____ Return equipment _____

Return filmstrip__Return slide__Return records__Return film__

The church should keep equipment locked up to insure safety and to guarantee that it has been inspected when returned and put away ready for immediate use.

A large calendar with small numbers and with sufficient white space on each day for listing equipment and materials will readily inform the person booking the equipment and the material, as well as those making requests, of what has already been scheduled for use. The Sunday area should be kept large, for it will probably be the day when materials are used most.

AN AUDIO-VISUAL CALENDAR

Sunday	Monday	Tuesday	Wednesday	Thursday	Friday	Saturday
1	2	3	4	5	6	7
8	9	10	11	12	13	14
15	16	17	18	19	20	21
22	23	24	25	26	27	28
29	30	31				

How to Get Started

The first responsibility of the audio-visual committee will be to take an inventory of surroundings, and of all audio-visual materials, resources, and equipment. The committee could begin by touring the entire church and church school. Note should be taken of the furniture, the fixtures, and the cleanliness of the rooms. Questions like these need to be answered: Is this room a good visual? Have the flags been cleaned since the last war? How old and frayed and soiled are the hangings in the room? Are there any poorly mounted or discolored pictures on the walls? Are they meaningful and placed at the eye level of the persons who use the room the most? What are those items on top of the piano? Play it! Does it sound like a piano or an untuned harpsichord? When was the room painted last? Are the walls and ceiling colors conducive to good learning? How could the room be darkened enough for good projection? Are there any outlets near the place where the projector should be placed? Other questions will suggest themselves to the committee.

Next, the committee members will want to don aprons or workclothes and search the closets, attics, and basement for equipment purchased in the first flush of the romantic age of audio-visuals. One will find good classroom use for even some old, low-wattage, 2" x 2" slide and filmstrip projectors. The motion picture projector may be quite a good instrument, needing a little oil, cleaning, projection lamp, or exciter lamp. Little can be done to recondition a screen that has become moldy because it has been left in a damp place. If forgotten and unused flat pictures are found, have the children's division leader of the church school examine them and determine if they are still usable.

In your search you may come upon a real archeological find in the estimation of some in this movie-minded age. A long black

99

object or a big bulky instrument may be located. The former will undoubtedly be a 3¼" x 4" standard stereopticon glass slide projector, and the latter will be an opaque projector. The committee will find use for both; so haul both out, dust them off, clean them up, use them, and house them in the new A-V center.

Finding a place in the church and equipping it so that a committee may function there will be the next responsibility. The audio-visual office should be centrally located, near the church office and not too far from any department of the church.

Films, filmstrips, and records should be kept in a dry place. The church should build or purchase from the local dealer efficient and adequate files to house filmstrips and scripts, as well as records. The materials should be cataloged and arranged so that they are readily accessible. Local church users of audio-visuals or committee members will not be so versatile as librarians are with books. Filmstrips should be kept in file drawers of low depth and in alphabetical order. Scripts should be kept in file drawers a little larger than 8½" x 11" (the usual size of script paper).

Having made a physical inventory, the committee will be ready to plan a first-year budget. The beginning budget will

need to be based on available materials and equipment, needs as discovered by a study of the total church program, the interest of teachers and leaders, and available funds.

An annual budget should include the following:

.Repair and/or replacement of equipment
New equipment
Servicing of equipment
Purchase of filmstrips
Purchase of films
Purchase of sound filmstrips
Rental of films
Rental of sound filmstrips
Purchase of magnetic tape, wall pictures, poster material, paints, crayons, clay, and other materials
Postage, paper, carbon paper, order forms
Visual Education Fellowship membership fee[3]
Printed resources—magazines, books, catalogs, guides to films

If there is a central church treasury, one can write into the total church budget an amount for audio-visuals. But the church will still need to allocate that budget amount to the various departments and organizations. In working out the solution, bear in mind that those who have the least money and the least voice in church matters may be in need of the most audio-visual materials. One should budget and allocate according to need. If there is no central treasury, the invoices would be referred to the proper department or organization for payment.

Selection and Evaluation of A-V Materials

It is usually impossible for most local church leaders to preview audio-visuals at their film library because most committees

---

[3] Write to your denomination or the National Council of Churches for information.

do not have a library nearby. But local church leaders are not without help in this regard. The major cooperating Protestant denominations have evaluated most of the audio-visual materials thought to be of potential value to the church. These evaluations are available in an *Audio-Visual Resource Guide* of the department of audio-visual and broadcast education, Division of Christian Education of the National Council of the Churches of Christ in the U.S.A. In addition to the guide, evaluations and news containing descriptions of new materials and recent developments in the field of audio-visuals are printed in the *International Journal of Religious Education*.

Also denominational supply houses, and the cooperative audio-visual library system known as Religious Film Libraries, issue catalogs containing a guide to films, with evaluations on which one can depend. A leader or teacher should not use a projected audio-visual without either previewing it or basing his selection on the evaluation and recommendation of a reliable source.

It is possible to arrive at some idea of the value of an audio-visual on the basis of past experience with libraries, film producers' products, and various ratings. We will need to remember, however, that evaluations are made out of the background and experience of the persons doing the rating. Their theology, denominational practice, and churchmanship color their appraisals. The technical quality, the purpose of the producer, and the persons for whom the film was made are also important factors. A producer issuing a film for general use is under some necessity to generalize and make his film palatable for as many users as possible. In every case it would be well to remember (1) that the producer's best intentions may not have got into the film; (2) that we can't always be sure of our audio-visual even with the best of recommendations; (3) that much depends on the rating given by the film librarian; (4) that we must analyze all advertisements, even those of our own denomination;

(5) that the person ordering and using the audio-visual could have a bias also; and (6) that we must become acquainted with the type of products issued by all producers.

Edgar Dale has given some clear guides for the selection and evaluation of audio-visual materials in the field of education:[4]

» Do the materials give a true picture of the ideas they present?
» Do they contribute meaningful content to the topic under study?
» Is the material appropriate for the age, intelligence, and experience of the learners?
» Is the physical condition of the materials satisfactory?
» Is there a teacher's guide available to provide help in the effective use of the materials?
» Do they make the students better thinkers, more critical-minded?
» Do they tend to improve human relations?
» Is the material worth the time, expense, and effort involved?

The Christian church would want to add the following:

» Will the theological position on which the audio-visual is based contribute to our learning?
» Are the teachings in accord with the basic beliefs held by our church?
» Will the material (with proper use) make a positive contribution to our Christian faith?

---

[4] *Audio-Visual Methods in Teaching* (Revised), by Edgar Dale. The Dryden Press, 1954. Quoted by permission.

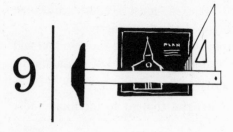

9

Rooms and Equipment to Fit Your Needs

❧ ❧ THERE ARE OVER 300,000 Protestant churches in the United States of America. Two thirds of them were planned and erected before the last two decades, when the use of audio-visuals received such great impetus. Unless your church was built recently it is probably not adapted in its present condition to the use of audio-visuals. There will be no shades to darken the room. Electrical outlets in which to plug in projectors will be misplaced or at a minimum. Electrical cords will be too light to carry the load. There will be no reading lamp for the script reader. Equipment will be ancient and inadequate. Fifteen years ago some churches used 100-watt slide and filmstrip projectors to project black and white filmstrips. Today the density of most color filmstrips has been increased to where best projection is obtained by the use of a 500-watt projector.

Even if a church was built a number of years ago and was not well arranged or equipped for the use of audio-visuals, it is still possible to make it functional. The cost of making minimum alterations would not be excessive. The purchase and installation of electrical outlets, blackout curtains, cabinets, and flat wall pictures could be made at a nominal cost. A start might be made by doing one room. Then eventually alterations could be made in the entire church.

Rooms are audio-visuals. Too many church rooms are objectionable visually. They are cluttered with curriculum materials. Furniture does not fit pupils. Color schemes clash. Pictures are hung too high, and they are hung too long. Flags go uncleaned.

Cleanliness, color, furniture arrangement, and adequate space, when given consideration in relation to each other and to one's purpose, can help make for a pleasant experience and a favorable learning situation.

Rooms should be kept clean, every inch of them. Accessible cabinets and storage space for all audio-visual equipment can be had. All materials used in the church should be put away after they have been used. If there are not enough cabinets or sufficient storage space, arrange to have more purchased or constructed.

Rooms have sound. While making a motion picture recently, we recorded some room sound to bridge the gaps between segments of narration on a film made in that room. Rooms talk, and often they talk too loudly or less eloquently than we realize.

Acoustics are important. The church, be it represented by pupil or teacher, pastor or laymen, has something important to say. It should be heard. Whether the speaker be a person or a mechanism that transmits sound from records, tape, or film, listeners should hear distinctly and without distortion. Hard-surfaced rooms will tend to sound harsh and metallic. They will tend to produce echoes making for inaudible sounds. When the acoustics of a room are less than the best, even the pleasantest of voices telling the best of stories, or the finest projection equipment using the latest in a sound film, will lose in quality. If one has difficulty with sound in any of the church rooms, an architect or a sound engineer should be consulted.

If plans are being made for a new building or major alterations, one should consult the denominational bureau of church building or write the Department of Church Building of the National Council of Churches of Christ in the U.S.A.

Whether one is remodeling or planning a new building, he should bear in mind the following fairly standard floor space requirements that are meeting with increasing general acceptance by the major Protestant denominations.

When planning rooms and equipment for the whole program of the whole church, one must plan for the use of audio-visuals too. Some time ago certain budget-minded leaders were suggesting one audio-visual room especially equipped and available to several departments or the total church school. But Christian education leaders have constantly held out for adequate space and suitable facilities for each department. They have not wanted a special room. Experience has proved that the ideal they espoused was valid and attainable.

The audio-visual technicians have constantly urged teachers to equip each teaching room adequately. Experiences in a number of churches have now shown that the availability of materials and the accessibility of equipment go hand in hand with the frequent and superior use of audio-visuals. Previously, when children were transferred to an audio-visual room, time, always at a premium, was wasted, the mood of the moment was lost, and the remainder of the church school was disturbed. If audio-visuals are integral to teaching, they need to be integrated time-wise and room-wise as well.

Every church should begin now to install basic equipment in classrooms and departments of the church school. This is the ideal plan. Every unit of the church school, primary age up, with more than thirty persons in attendance, should have a record player, a slide and filmstrip projector, and a screen available in the room at all times. The equipment should be set up in position ready for use. A wall screen, covered by drapes that can

STANDARD FLOOR SPACE REQUIREMENTS

Age Group	Pupils per Room	Space per Person
NURSERY I and II Ages 1½-2	10-15	35 sq. ft.—good 30 sq. ft.—fair under 25 sq. ft.—poor.
NURSERY III Age 3	Up to 15—good 15-18—fair more than 18—poor.	35 sq. ft.—good 30 sq. ft.—fair under 25 sq. ft.—poor.
KINDERGARTEN I and II Ages 4, 5	20 pupils—good 20-25—fair over 25—poor.	35 sq. ft.—good 30 sq. ft.—fair under 25 sq. ft.—poor.
PRIMARY I, II, and III Ages 6, 7, 8—Grades 1, 2, 3	Up to 25 pupils per room. Up to 45, three rooms; one larger for assembly at times.	20-30 sq. feet
JUNIOR I, II, and III Ages 9, 10, 11—Grades 4, 5, 6	Up to 45 pupils, three rooms; one larger for assembly at times.	20-30 sq. feet
JUNIOR HIGH I, II, III Ages 12, 13, 14—Grades 7, 8, 9	20 pupils—maximum.	15-18 sq. ft.—good 12-15 sq. ft.—fair 10-12 sq. ft.—poor.
SENIOR HIGH & OLDER YOUTH Ages 15, 16, 17—Grades 9, 10, 11 Ages 18-23 (older youth)	25 pupils—maximum.	15-18 sq. ft.—good 12-15 sq. ft.—fair 10-12 sq. ft.—poor.
ADULTS Ages 19-24 (young adults) Ages 40-64 (adults) Age 65 yrs. up (older adults)	Not over 50 pupils per room.	Lecture type—8-10 sq. ft. Activity type—10-12 sq. ft.

107

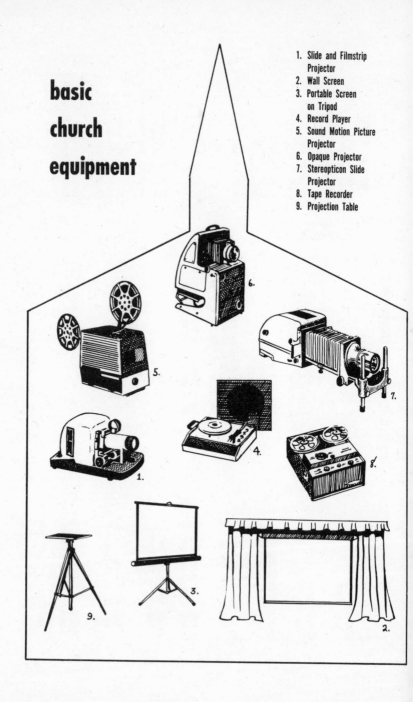

basic church equipment

1. Slide and Filmstrip Projector
2. Wall Screen
3. Portable Screen on Tripod
4. Record Player
5. Sound Motion Picture Projector
6. Opaque Projector
7. Stereopticon Slide Projector
8. Tape Recorder
9. Projection Table

be drawn aside at a moment's notice, and equipment that need not be booked and carried from a library, will stimulate a greater use of audio-visuals. The church audio-visual library should be accessible and staffed to insure its being open when a teacher wishes to get material.

What equipment should a church purchase? How should the purchase be planned? Who should authorize the expenditure of funds for audio-visuals? Who will purchase? Shall the several pieces of equipment be purchased at the same time? Where should the money be obtained?

Experience has proved the advisability of following these basic principles in purchasing equipment:

» Purchase slowly and with care.

» Purchase standard equipment locally.

» Purchase in relationship to future growth.

» Purchase cabinets or arrange for storage space.

» Purchase in keeping with need.

» Purchase as interest and use warrant.

» Purchase in relationship to budget.

» Remember to budget for rentals.

Under no circumstances should the minister buy audio-visual equipment and materials in order to get the church started. Nor should equipment be borrowed from even the best church member. There is danger that he will operate and control what may become a sort of one-man show in the church.

Audio-visual equipment is expensive. A congregation will understand that a slide and filmstrip projector may cost over $100. They may accept the fact that a 16-mm. sound motion picture projector will cost more than $500. But they will not understand that the sound projector requires much more money for the rental of films. Users of audio-visual materials with local church responsibility must educate their constituency about continuing costs. Filmstrips cost money. Slides cost money. Films are expensive to rent and much more expensive to purchase. As one budgets for equipment, so one must educate one's constituency to plan for the purchase of materials to use in the equipment.

Most churches have found it advisable to purchase first a 2" x 2" slide and filmstrip projector and a screen. In the average-size church where one such projector must serve both large and small groups, it would be well to obtain a 500-watt projector. The projector should be easy to thread and allow for turning back readily to a previously projected frame. The lamp and lens system should give a sharp picture over the entire screen, and with little distortion between the amount of light projected against the outside of the screen as opposed to the light provided at the center. A denominational audio-visual dealer, or a local dealer who keeps abreast of audio-visual equipment and the needs of the church, should be consulted.

The screen should always be kept high enough so that a person in the back can see the entire screen over the heads of persons in front. This may be done by staggering chairs so that viewers can see between the heads of persons in the front row. Or else raise screen and projector high enough to enable all viewers to see the entire screen regardless of how persons are seated. Seating an audience for purposes of viewing a projected picture on a screen is best done in a long, narrow room. The accompanying chart illustrates this. Beaded screens give the clearest picture in a long, narrow room, for the light from a beaded screen is reflected back directly toward its source. Persons seated ten feet or more from the screen, outside the area marked in the drawing (45-degree angle from the center of the screen), will find the image somewhat distorted or faded and its sharpness lost. It is better to arrange it so that the audience may be seated straight back from the screen, but not too far on either side, particularly at the front.

As budgeting and proper use can be assured, the church will want to install permanent wall screens in all rooms and cover them with drapes that may be readily and easily drawn when the screen is used. The general rule for determining screen size is that the width of the screen should be about one-sixth the distance from the screen to the last row of seats. A wall screen in a room with a depth of sixty feet would call for a screen approximately ten feet wide.

Wall screens are usually permanently installed. But if the hangings are standardized, wall screens semipermanently installed may on occasion be moved to another room. Such a procedure, however, defeats the basic principles of the availability and accessibility of equipment. If one must make multi-

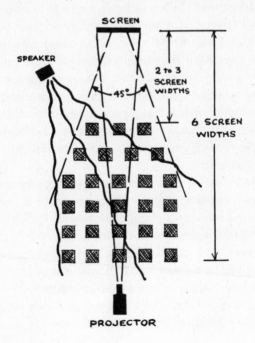

SCREEN

SPEAKER

2 to 3
SCREEN
WIDTHS

45°

6 SCREEN
WIDTHS

PROJECTOR

purpose use of the screen, it would be better to purchase a 70" x 70" screen on a tripod. It will need to be large enough for the largest group and be easily transported to various rooms in the church. Screens should be rolled up after use. If a screen is used outdoors, especially in summer, it should be rolled up indoors where one can see that no butterflies or lightning bugs have been trapped, for crushing them in the rolled-up screen may stain it.

If budget permits, one may wish to install a large electrically operated screen in the sanctuary and in the main church hall. Both should be so recessed that at no time is there interference with worship or church programming. Screens would rarely be used in the sanctuary during the day. But many evening services lend themselves to the use of films and filmstrips. Care should be taken to begin darkening the room first and then rolling the screen into position. When done this way in a service of worship or a well-integrated verbal presentation, there will be no break in the mood of the participating group. The procedure should be reversed at the close of the visual presentation.

Next, one will want to purchase a three- or four-speed record player of a standard make. Recordings and transcriptions ought to be reproduced with as fine a quality instrument as the church can afford. High quality instruments should always be purchased. The best of programs may be ruined by the use of inferior equipment.

The third piece of equipment purchased may be the 16-mm. sound motion picture projector. Again, it would be well to purchase it from one's own church audio-visual agency or from a local recognized dealer. One will want to purchase from a dealer who is expected to stay in business, who can service the equipment, and who will stand by his claims. It is advisable to have one or more persons on the audio-visual committee who knows every feature of the equipment. It is a great convenience to have a projection table on rollers for use with heavy equipment.

All equipment should be standard. No one manufacturing concern is necessarily better than another. Products of a given concern vary some in quality from year to year. Purchasers should test each model in terms of performance and ease of operation. They should insist on lightness and durability. Most projectors today are fairly light, need oiling infrequently, and are fairly quiet in operation. Sound projectors can be purchased as single units, with the speaker built into or attached to the face of the projector, or as two separate units. One must be sure to have at least a 15-watt output of sound for large halls. Although classrooms may require less output of sound, the multipurpose use of what amounts to one sound projector in a local church would require the all-purpose (regular 15-watt output of sound) equipment.

A speaker for a sound motion picture projector should be placed on a level and to one side of the screen. But in a room where acoustics are a problem one may need to experiment with placing the speaker in any one of several positions or places—in a corner, the rear of the room, high or low. It goes without saying that the equipment should be in first-class working order. It is well to remember that even the newest churches sometimes have a problem with acoustics.

One should buy an extra bulb for each projector owned by the church and have on hand such extra items as exciter lamps, fuses, magnetic tape, and pulley belts for all equipment. Electrical cords of standard size should be used. The location of electrical outlets in relation to placement of equipment will determine the length of the electrical cords and the number needed. If possible, long cords should be avoided by installing additional outlets.

Film for church use in the sound motion picture projector comes in 16-mm. size. Theaters use 35-mm. film, and there is 8-mm. film for use in small projectors in homes. In this book we are concerned with 16-mm. film. Motion picture film is measured by the foot. At present, a reel of 16-mm. film consists of 400 feet, approximately. It requires fifteen minutes to show one reel of silent film, and eleven minutes to show a reel of sound film. The difference in time is due to the fact that the sound film must run through the projector faster to get the proper sound reproduction. A spool for 400 feet of film (one reel) measures seven inches in diameter. In sound film, longer subjects are wound on larger spools. A large spool may carry as many as five reels of film. There are larger spools, but most projector arms holding the larger-than-five-reel spools do not extend far enough from the projector to allow the larger spools to pass.

Some time after the purchase of the slide and filmstrip projector and the motion picture projector, the church should have the committee examine the opaque projector, the tape recorder, and either a projection stand or a portable projection table.

The opaque projector is a simple device to operate. It is an effective teaching tool. Any object not more than an inch in thickness, and less than the size of a regular sheet of typing paper, may be placed in the newer-make projector. By a process of using mirrors and a lamp, the image of the object is reflected through a lens and projected against a screen. Books may be placed in the projector and a page projected, thus enlarging type, charts, maps, and figures. The opaque projector can be used to project flat pictures, hymns from a hymnbook, illustrations from books, maps, and objects. In short, one can project any opaque material no larger than the size indicated above.

An opaque projector may be used to present information (pictures, figures, charts) singly or in sequence for the whole class to view. As with all projected material it calls for a concentration of attention on the part of the whole viewing group. Total blackout is required for good projection. Flat pictures may be pasted or drawn on a roll of paper. Then each picture may be rolled into position for projection when needed. One may also place the pictures, if they are thin enough, on top of each other and simply pull the last projected picture out when ready for the next one. Stagger each a little so one can get hold of them. This procedure provides for smoothness of operation, though one is limited to the number of pictures that can be placed in the projector. It is better to paste the pictures on a roll of paper and roll the sheet through from picture to picture.

An opaque projector may be used like a filmstrip projector to project pictures for worship, teaching a skill, showing a sequence, or the location of an event. The art work of children, young people, and adults may be projected on a screen with an opaque projector. It will have unlimited use. The only limiting factor will be the time and ingenuity of the leader and the class members. The best procedure would be to start personal and church files on all subjects generally accepted as the concern of the church. As the leader has guessed, the door is wide open; therefore, the best pictures one can find should be saved and filed for future use.

We would be remiss in our educational approach to the use of audio-visuals if mention were not made of the standard, $3\frac{1}{4}'' \times 4''$, stereopticon slide projector. The $3\frac{1}{4}'' \times 4''$ slide lends itself to creative use in the local church. Projects in Sunday, weekday, or vacation church school studies, calling for a visualization of a subject for the total group, may be designed and drawn in black and white or color on etched glass. The booklet *How to Make Hand-Made Lantern Slides*, and the necessary glass and crayons, may be ordered from the Keystone View Company, Meadville, Pennsylvania. Every child, or adult for that matter, may visualize by tracing or by free-hand drawing some phase of the unit of study under consideration. The story of what the group learned may then be projected as a series of slides on the standard $3\frac{1}{4}'' \times 4''$ projector. See pages 35, 36.

Tape recorders today are made to play at speeds of 1⅞, 3¾, 7½, or 15 inches per second. Protestant denominations issuing taped sound filmstrips or programs have conformed to the use of a 7½-inch per second speed. A tape recorder can be purchased for less than $100 or for more than $1000. The use to which it will be put, the necessity to transport the recorder, the number of persons using the equipment, and the quality of recording needed, plus budget, will help to determine what make and quality of equipment to purchase. For example, if the tape recorder is to be used to record the morning service and to be played back for the benefit of the sick and shut-ins, a less expensive instrument will do. If it is to be used to correct speech or voice defects of pastor, choir members, teachers, and superintendents, then it should reproduce those sounds with greater fidelity.

The opaque projector, the standard 3¼″ x 4″ slide projector, and the tape recorder are instruments requiring less money for use after purchase. One can make the materials to be used in them. Most other equipment requires a budget for the purchase and rental of films, filmstrips, and slides.

There are other types of audio-visual equipment which the church should have. Some have already been described in previous chapters. They include table-top easels to hold pictures for worship centers; easels for drawing; panels made of composition board placed about the room, on which children may hang or place pictures; a flannelgraph board and easel, as well as large storage space for cutouts.

Audio-Visuals Are Here to Stay

Audio-visuals are here to stay. They will be used to some degree in all church rooms and halls. Therefore, one should plan and build for permanent use. In some cases the darkening of a room can best be achieved by using shades that are opaque, with the prevailing color of the outside of the building on the outside surface, and dark green or black on the inside. If there is objection to using only dark shades, one may mount two shades in each window—the opaque one to be drawn only for projection purposes.

Today it is considered best to use full drapes at least half again as wide as the width of the window. They should be made of heavy cloth. The cloth can be purchased from theater supply houses. The drapes may be hung on a waxed rod and operated with pull-cords. They may be mounted inside the casement or on the face of the casement, depending on the particular types of windows they are mounted on as well as the kind of draperies used. The particular merit of traversing draperies is that in summer, with the windows open, they will let air in the room while at the same time, though they billow, keeping most of the light out. Summer heat will not be a problem in the future, however—more and more churches are being air-conditioned.

The color of the shades or drapes should harmonize with the color scheme of the room. Draperies add greatly to the beauty, charm, and homelikeness of a room and assist in reducing bad acoustical effects. Regardless of what kind of draperies are installed they should be kept fresh and clean.

A reading lamp may be made or purchased for use with reading scripts for filmstrips. Since many filmstrips still come with only one script, some system by which the script reader may signal the projectionist for a change of frame or slide should be arranged. The preview session is the time to practice this so there is smoothness of projection. The reader may wish to record the script on tape. Then the script will be available to the projectionist and no signaling system will be required. One should use a narrator with some ability, or see to it that the reader practices—enunciates clearly and pronounces correctly.

A beginning library of audio-visuals might well include high quality materials like the following, which may be ordered from any denominational audio-visual library.

Life of Christ—Elsie Anna Wood[1]
Life of Christ—Jacques Barosin[2]
Panorama of the Christian Church—Roland Bainton[3]

Christian Symbols[4]

The Life of Our Lord[5]

Life of Christ, Parts I and II—Barosin[2]

Jesus and the Disciples[6]

Palestine in Jesus' Day, Parts I and II[6]

The Growth in Our Idea of God[6]

The Bible Through the Centuries[6]

The Church in New Testament Times[6]

Two Thousand Years Ago[7]

Our Old Testament Heritage[6]

The Dead Sea Scrolls and Our Scriptures[8]

Amos—Barosin[4]

The History of the Christian Church Series[1]

Our Protestant Heritage[6]

---

[1] Produced by Society for Visual Education.

[2] Produced by the Evangelical and Reformed Church.

[3] Produced by the Yale Divinity School.

[4] Produced by Bureau of Audio-Visual Aids, Evangelical and Reformed Church.

[5] Matson Photo Service.

[6] Produced by the Evangelical and Reformed Church and Congregational Christian Churches.

[7] Produced by J. Arthur Rank.

[8] Produced by The Board of Christian Education and Publication of the Evangelical and Reformed Church in cooperation with the Bureau of Audio-Visual Aids.

In purchasing slides and filmstrips for the local church library, the committee should bear in mind several basic principles and procedures:

» Purchase repeat-use materials.

» Obtain these materials singly for a given use, unless the church has come into an inheritance and/or can get a bargain by buying several subjects. Beware, however, of stocking a library without adequately preparing persons to use the materials purchased.

» Purchase while planning the teaching.

» Order materials early enough for preview and proper integration.

» Plan six weeks in advance.

» Keep a balance in the material secured for the various age groups and organizations.

» Ask oneself if the material purchased is in keeping with the basic theological position of the church.

» One may want to study and view other materials but not purchase them.

» Purchase only high quality material.

» Do not purchase materials that violate the accepted educational procedures of our time. We refer here, particularly, to frightening people into faith or telling them into the kingdom.

Remember that church leaders are in competition with magazines using much color and with screen productions costing millions of dollars that too often surpass in excellence that which is used by the church. The church does not have the money to produce as high quality material as it would like. Any support one can give the church in this regard will benefit all teachers and leaders.

Slides have been supplanted by filmstrips to a large degree, but a library should have sets of slides on the life of Christ, the history of the local church, and many art masterpieces illustrating incidents and ideas in the Bible and in church history.

In most instances slides are made from original Kodachromes and therefore are second-generation products. They are photographed directly from the original. Filmstrips are made from negatives, which in turn were made from originals and therefore are third-generation products. There is a difference in quality between a second- and a third-generation product.

Slides allow for single use or a rearranging of scenes, whereas the sequence of scenes in a filmstrip cannot be changed. However, one can place one's hand over the lens and skip several frames (remember to count correctly) or cut up a filmstrip and bind the frames in single-frame glass binders. But the latter is not recommended for the following reasons:

(1) The filmstrip was designed for the consecutive use of scenes. To remove a few frames for use in slides would spoil the use of the remainder of the frames in the filmstrip.

(2) The slide made from a filmstrip and projected against a screen is of single-frame size and must be projected from the same distance as a filmstrip, thus giving less light on the screen. This factor, plus the aforementioned factor that it is a third-generation product, will lessen the quality of the image obtained.

(3) If certain frames in a filmstrip are so good that one will want slides made of them, the producer will, in all likelihood, make them from the original photographs or drawings on special order, thus allowing one to keep the filmstrip and at the same time maintain a higher quality picture through the use of the slide projected on the screen.

Before purchasing either slides or filmstrips, ascertain the quality of the materials and their general recommendation by your denomination or by united Protestantism through evaluation committees reporting under the auspices of the Department of Audio-Visual and Broadcast Education of the Division of Christian Education of the NCCCUSA. Such evaluations appear monthly in the *International Journal of Religious Education* and the annual *Audio-Visual Resource Guide*.

10

How to Write a Script

✠ ✠ SCRIPT-WRITING for filmstrips, sound filmstrips, or slide sets calls for some special skill. Script writers are not born. They get that way by accepting certain disciplines of hard work, much practice, and concentrated thinking. Anyone can learn to write scripts.

"The use of words, music, and sound effects with a picture or pictures is like bouncing a rubber ball off a billboard." So said the late Alan Shilin, writer and producer of more than a hundred films and writer of hundreds of filmstrip scripts for Protestant churches. He also added, "Script-writing requires an aesthetic touch, a plus element that lifts it above the ordinary."

What Is Script-Writing?

Script-writing is three-dimensional communication. Putting sound (voices, music, sound effects) and pictures together in such a way as to give a third-dimensional effect is the task of the script writer.

---

[1] The writer is indebted to the late Alan Shilin for much of what is contained in this chapter. Through his script-writing seminar at the International A-V Christian Education Workshop, his review of scripts, and his gracious, unselfish sharing, he has contributed greatly to what is said here.

VISUAL	AUDIO	
Picture or Illustration	Narration	Sound Effects
Describe pictures destined to be seen	Write words destined to be spoken and heard	Describe sound effects destined to be heard

When writing a "reading script" (narration read as pictures are projected) it is necessary to write only the first two columns. A writer should "listen" in his own mind as he writes. The script writer's success is measured by the skill with which he relates audio and visual. When these are well related a synthesis is produced. Script-writing is not a matter of addition. One and one do not make two. It is now a matter of multiplication.

Actually, this synthesis may be compared to a chord of music. A chord is a simultaneous combination of different sounds either consonant or dissonant. When audio and visual are well integrated in a frame or series of frames of a filmstrip a chord is produced. A chord in a filmstrip presents sight and sound in such a manner that the "hearer-viewer" gets one impact, one sensation, one thought.

The script writer must think and plan in terms of an audio-visual chord. He cannot think of picture alone or of narration (or other sound) alone. He sees and hears at the same time. There are situations where visual or audio is stronger and therefore one may take precedence over the other. One word may be all that's needed to complete the chord when the visual says it. A picture of a thin, pot-bellied child hardly needs words for the audio portion of the chord. One word, "starving," would suffice.

When the script writer adds not just a good voice but the right kind of voice, plus the right color picture, music, and sound effects, the result is a unit of sensations, an audio-visual chord that is effective. Using a series of these chords in proper sequence and building to a clear climax is the script writer's task.

The picture column is the tyrant. The script writer who can design the slide set or filmstrip from its inception may choose the scenes he wishes to present and write to them. Thus he may review what he has written and alter descriptions of scenes repeatedly until the script moves from a catchy beginning through to the conclusion without at any time losing his audience. Such a script is an effective script.

Becoming a Script Writer

You, the reader of these pages, can become a script writer. If you are interested and are willing to work, you can write scripts. A technical background is not needed. Rid yourself of any fears you may have developed about its unknown demands. True, script-writing may be a new medium for you, but it does not require a genius.

Church people, as well as any other people, can write scripts. To do so we would suggest that you study some good scripts. Analyze them. Make note of the beginning and ending, the chords, the sequence, the transitions. Notice the sentences, phraseology, single words, or even the sounds that may be used with certain frames. Then practice writing. Read billboard ads. Read captions in the picture magazines. Complete sentences may not be needed. The picture may suggest more than half the sentence, so that all that is needed is one word, but the selection of the right word is important.

Procedure in Script-Writing

(1) *State the purpose or theme.* Aim to do something with the potential viewer-hearer group. Remember that the simple theme is the best. It is an artist's responsibility to "make the

most out of the least." Also, ask yourself the question: Does the theme I have chosen lend itself easily to pictorial treatment?

(2) *Choose your art medium.* Photographs, art drawings, and cartoons are the basic media of visualization in filmstrips. Budget generally determines the quality and standard used, but subject matter and the purpose of the filmstrip should determine the medium. One should select the medium that can be exploited most in the interest of an effective filmstrip. Illustrations should be chosen that are in keeping with the spirit, purpose, and mission of the material.

Art drawings "manufacture" a picture according to previously agreed-upon specifications. One can include details and eliminate nonessentials more easily in art drawings than in other media. Anything that is happening today or tomorrow can be photographed, but everything that has already happened must be drawn, or staged and photographed. The latter is expensive and time-consuming, whereas the contribution of the artist is almost limitless in art illustration. He is bound only by his own imagination and ability. He can give the picture subtleties that enlarge its dimension. For example, it is to be noted that *Life*, a picture magazine primarily devoted to photographs, presented the story of primitive man with drawings.

Cartoons are used to generalize. They are indefinite. Cartoon characters can be anyone or everyone. No one thinks that the cartoon figure's predicament refers to himself until he is taken in with the lesson or message. A good cartoon is a drawing stripped to its barest elements. It tells you the story at a glance, without subtleties, usually with lightness and humor.

It is best to use photographs for contemporary reporting. They are the documentary medium. Visualizing the present-day activity of real people in real places demands this particular medium. Most filmstrips are now made in color, but black and white should be used when grim facts and stark reality without frills are wanted. The colored dress of an underprivileged Oriental may belie his poverty, whereas black and white may better convey the bleakness of his situation.

It is better not to mix media in a given filmstrip, but if necessary it should be done in a pattern that justifies itself to the audience and is intelligible to them.

(3) *Choose the characters* who will carry the action of your story. People are interested in other people. Following persons with whom one is in sympathy heightens the interest of a story. If a writer can tell a story without the personal element, it may be that some medium other than a filmstrip would serve his purpose better. A *Puppy for Jose*[1] and *Brothers All*[2] are examples of filmstrips with personalized plots.

(4) *Gather facts.* Remember that the writer need be only fairly well informed on the subject. Contrary to common belief one does not need to know all about the subject on which one is writing. Many a script writer has failed because he knew a great deal and thought that his particular script should contain most of it. It is important not to be encyclopedic! But it is also important to present the truth.

(5) *Write a brief synopsis of the plot*, and perhaps diagram it as a means of visualizing your plot. Every filmstrip must have three parts: a beginning, a middle, and an ending. A situation is established, something happens to alter or upset it, and there is a resolution of the situation. Your synopsis and diagram should show at least these three parts.

(6) *Write a rough draft of the script*, beginning with any portion that comes to you the most easily. If desired, fill in the picture descriptions as you go along; otherwise complete the descriptions later. Do not stop to polish rough spots and smooth transitions. Be chiefly concerned about the question, "What

---

[1] Produced by Friendship Press.
[2] Produced by Christian Education Press.

shall be said about this big idea?" Later rearrange and edit the material to reach that cherished goal called effectiveness. Proceeding in this way lessens the likelihood of losing important ideas.

In writing your rough draft, confine the story to the present unless you cannot do otherwise. It is best to proceed forward, for that's the way most people move mentally and physically. The process of beginning with a frame of the present and then going back twenty years and ending with the beginning frame in the present is described as a flashback. Flashback technique is second best. When a whole filmstrip is a flashback, it is equivalent to action in the present.

Write simply and briefly, avoiding professional jargon. No one listens to professional talk anyway except another professional, and he isn't the person one wants to reach. Write in ordinary, everyday language because that's what people understand. Too much alliteration, too many clichés, triteness, and the repetition of catchy phrases are evils of professionalism. The writer will, however, try to be versatile with synonyms. No reader should ever allow an unknown word to walk by him without examining it carefully in a dictionary. Education in the use of words is a continuing process.

The use of humor in your script-writing once in a while helps to make the people in your story human. Humor, like mistakes, errors in judgment and failures, increases opportunities of identification. Members of the audience will recognize themselves in a script containing humor.

(7) *Rework your material to establish sequences,* polishing the narration and completing the visualization, or picture descriptions, as needed. In picture parlance a *sequence* refers to a series of shots of persons or things made at varying distances and angles. The subject matter is viewed "from all sides." The several frames of the sequence are held together by the content of the subject matter.

In writing the visualization for a sequence the writer should begin with an *establishing shot* to tell the audience what they are going to see. This is usually a *long shot* (LS) encompassing enough to give locale, mood, and action at a glance. Or a *close-up* (CU), an intimate view, could be used as the establishing shot if it includes some identifying element or symbol, such as a surgical instrument if the location is a hospital. The writer will seek for the type of establishing shot that best suits his purpose. By the use of the proper establishing shot, every member of the viewing group should be put in the mood of the filmstrip. Sometimes it is necessary to use several frames for the establishing sequence.

In developing his sequence the writer should remember that the element of surprise is a great asset in holding audiences. People can be caught off guard with pictures. Moving from a long shot to a medium (MS) to a close shot (CS), followed by a medium shot, an extreme close-up or a medium shot from a unique angle can jolt an audience into attention. People like the intimate shot, the close-up. Much photography by amateurs presents the whole person, including shoes and hat, when in reality audiences want to know who persons are and how they are reacting by seeing close views of their faces. The *cut-away*,

also, is a device that can be used to add interest to a sequence. Looking at the same scene too long causes eye-strain. A cut-away to an object with which actors are concerned releases the grip time makes on viewers. A cut-away from a general meeting, for example, to individual persons or objects allows the script writer to complete his sequence without losing his group. Looking at a person from a high or a low angle are other types of shots or angles that a writer could ask for when writing a script. A tall person will look taller if seen from a low angle and will appear shorter if photographed or drawn from a high angle. Beware, however, of venturing into too many photographic or art extremes. The unusual angles and dramatic shots should be used only when they will actually assist you in saying something important. As in baseball, remember to "save the best pitch for the time it will do the most good."

When dialogue is used in the script, it is important to remember that the best illusion can be created from the picture accompanying it by focusing attention on the listener rather than on the speaker, who should be pictured from a side view or a rear view. Let us not show a speaker in a still picture with his mouth open!

When the art medium for a filmstrip is photography, the photographer will want to provide the filmstrip editor with some *fluidity* in the selection of pictures. Fluidity is obtained by taking several shots from a variety of angles. A scene may be re-enacted or re-staged for the additional shots. The additional shots will enable the editor to *match frames*, thus providing for better transitions from frame to frame.

Variety in the script itself can be secured by striving to achieve a broken pattern in writing. An effect of surprise may be obtained, for example, by allotting the usual amount of text to a medium shot but only one to three words of script to a close-up. Remember, too, that the picture limits the number of words to be used and that too many words slow down the pace of a filmstrip. About twenty-five words per frame is a good average length for a script; if the script seems too long in some places and cannot be condensed, a medium shot and a close-up of the same picture could be used. Narration should be brief as a telegram is brief. It should embellish and undergird pictures, not describe them. It should multiply the effectiveness of the visual by adding a word, a phrase, a sentence or two. Words and pictures should complement each other, not duplicate each other.

(8) The script writer should grasp attention with each frame and propel the group forward frame after frame, sequence after sequence. Such a bridge could be made with words, with pictures, or both. Usually the last scene of a preceding sequence could establish in part the one that is to follow. Word transitions can be made with divided sentences or by the repetition of a word or a phrase. Frames 8-17 of the sound filmstrip *Do You Dig Friendship?* offer an example of bridges with words.

8. FOUR KIDS DRINKING OUT OF ONE SODA, ALL OBVIOUSLY HAPPY AND ENJOYING ONE AN-OTHER'S COMPANY
   Everyone was havin' a ball!

9. MORE KIDS DRINKING OUT OF SODA
   Everyone was havin' a ball!

10. STILL MORE KIDS DRINKING OUT OF SODA
    Everyone . . .

11. SEYMOUR ALONE WITH HIS SODA
    . . . (groan) . . . well, almost everyone.

12. CLOSE-UP OF SEYMOUR
    The trouble with Seymour was that he didn't dig friendship. Wherever Seymour went . . .

13. SEYMOUR ALONE AT FOOTBALL GAME
    . . . the football games . . .

14. SEYMOUR SEATED HOLDING FLOWER
      . . . the school dances . . .

15. SEYMOUR ALONE AT THE BEACH
      . . . the beach . . . he was always alone.

16. SEYMOUR IGNORED AT THE BEACH BY THE
    GIRLS
      The girls just didn't know he was alive . . .

17. SEYMOUR IGNORED BY THE BOYS
      . . . and neither did the fellows.

A handy mechanical procedure to follow when doing a script would be as follows:

List numbers spaced every four lines on paper equal to the number of frames planned. A pencil or ink line can be drawn across the paper at each number. This line and what you eventually write on it will describe and represent your picture. The space beneath it is for your script. (Or use two columns—audio and visual.) Then fill in the frames that are to become the title, credit, and end frames and write in the narration of your filmstrip on the remaining lines.

(9) If your filmstrip is a sound filmstrip, add music and/or sound effects as desired and needed.

One should remember that in a sound filmstrip one has a constant ally, the narrator. He can be the writer's greatest friend, when he has been chosen for quality of voice, ability in timing and so on; otherwise he can be the writer's worst enemy. The voice can add meaning and dramatic effect to words. The voice, enunciation, inflections, and timing can make the difference between an effective and an ineffective presentation. If a second or a third voice is used in your sound filmstrip, remember that it is good form to begin and end with the same voice.

Music is often used to begin and end sound filmstrips. At the beginning, as with the establishing shot in pictures, it can help to set the mood for the story to be told, and at the end it can bring the story to an artistic close.

Music can also serve as a bridge to connect scenes and sequences. It can make transition between the mood of one sequence to the mood of the next. It can assist the narrator in giving the proper pacing to the various frames of a filmstrip, giving forward movement or slowing down the pace, to allow the pictures time to do their work.

Pauses in the narrative are also dramatic devices for a story and should be used more frequently than they are. Have you ever had the sight of some breath-taking mountain view diluted by the words of an overzealous conversationalist? There are pictures that speak for themselves, to which words cannot add but only detract. Music can be used to multiply the message of a picture during such a pause in the narrative. It can supply much-needed "open spaces" to a script.

The script writer himself can do some of his own research in the music to be used. He can choose the one or two compositions that are to begin and end his story. For the main body of his material, however, he should bear in mind that visual presentations usually do not require music with form. For example, a hymn tune which is completely familiar to hearers should not be used unless specifically needed, since familiar tunes divert attention instead of strengthening the presentation. Music should be chosen on the basis of its power to evoke the particular emotions or ideas demanded by the script.

(10) When your script is complete and all your art work is at hand, *re-edit your material thoroughly*, asking yourself the following questions:

» Is the writing simple and as brief as possible?

» Does the art work fulfill the visualization as originally planned?
» Is there adequate variety in the art work and the script?
» Do the frames move into each other with sufficient smoothness?

Working with Slides

Sometimes the would-be writer has his art work already in hand before he begins his script. It is miscellaneous material that needs to be organized and integrated, the art medium of which is usually slides.

Slides may be "worked with" (viewed, interchanged, discarded) as one writes a script. You can make your own slide-viewing apparatus, using a piece of glass salvaged from an old windowpane or other transparent material. Strips of wood to serve as guide lines and as supports may be glued horizontally across the transparent material, spaced a little over 2″ apart, or a little more than the width of the slide. The glass is then placed on a table or desk at a sloping angle with a light behind it. The slides are placed on the glass and culled and sorted into several piles—excellent, medium, and poor. The poor slides should be disposed of quickly. One should select about 60-100 excellent-medium slides. Then they may be reduced in number to within twenty-five frames of the filmstrip length. In the process of selection and culling the writer will become acquainted with the slides.

The slides should be gone over again and again until they begin to fit into patterns. Either the mind of the narrator (writer) or the visual in the slides will be the cohesive factor. It could be both.

The most effective slides should be placed on the lower portion of the glass and the others toward the top as the writer rearranges them. Introductory slides should go to the top. As one works them over and thinks about the purpose and germ ideas that have already suggested themselves, a pattern and general sequence will come to mind. One should not be disturbed or disappointed if this comes hard the first time. Walk away, forget the pictures and come back the next day to start again.

When ideas come to the writer they should be written down in the form in which they came. They may be corrected and rearranged later. It is always good to stress the big ideas, the big issues. One should not try to become an authority but instead just tell a simple story with one basic impact or message. A filmstrip is being written, not a tome. One is reaching persons with a simple message, supported and augmented by a unique combination of words and pictures.

Write your script over! Practice! Persist in writing, and you will eventually be able to write effective scripts.

11 |

Audio-Visuals and Worship

✣ ✣ WORSHIP is a unique experience. It involves the whole man—body, mind, and spirit. All emotions, all responses, all faculties, all interests are included. The inner man, the outer man, the upper reaches and the lower reaches are brought together before God. Through adoration and praise, confession and forgiveness, thanksgiving and petition, confession of faith, consecration and benediction, man worships. All these elements are basic to worship, but not every service of worship need include all.

In worship great spiritual drives are released. Life's horizons are made broader. One's scale of values becomes truer. In worship one comes to belong to a new community, an inner fellowship.

True worship results in more than an emotional experience. True worship also involves the intellect and the will. Worship is the most basic means available for changing human nature or transforming character. Worship taps the deeper levels of our spiritual insight. It brings man in closer harmony with the infinite. Man communes with God.

With this general concept of worship in mind, limited though the statement may be, let us discover what contribution audio-visuals may make to worship, some of the common hurdles one must overcome, and the great experiences that may be had. In addition, this chapter will include several services illustrating the contributions audio-visuals may make to worship.

Audio-visuals used in worship will enhance that experience in a unique manner.

» *They can focus attention.* Audio-visuals "force" the worshiper to concentrate. This is true when a picture is viewed in a darkened room.

» *They can create an atmosphere.* Audio-visuals help establish a climate with unity, oneness, and a sense of communion. A well-lighted flat picture and quiet music create an atmosphere. So do objects, projected still pictures, and motion pictures.

» *They can clear the mind.* Audio-visuals, in a limited sense, direct our thoughts. They remove inhibitions and fears. Thus one sings more lustily when words to a song are projected on a screen. The room is dark, and people are not afraid to sing.

» *They can stir the emotions.* Audio-visuals create feelings of pleasure, pain, grief, joy, and astonishment. They move the mind and soul.

» *They can lift the spirit.* Audio-visuals exalt. They cause us to wonder. They create a sense of awe. They take us outside ourselves and away from ourselves. They open the "heart." They help establish a mood.

Audio-visuals may make all these contributions in services of worship, but one will need to plan the services carefully. Much work will need to be done. Sincere sensitivity is required of the leader and participants. Careful preparation and skilled leadership are needed if persons are to worship. Worship does not happen easily or readily no matter whether one uses silence, words, or word pictures.

The use of audio-visuals in worship is extremely difficult. Objects can get between the worshipers and God. Pictures, machines, and symbols may interfere with continuity. Thinking may be stopped or diverted. The ascent of the spirit may be halted.

Certain precautions need to be taken. It is better not to have people stand during a visual worship service unless it has been predetermined that the worshiper's view of the visual will not be blocked. One cannot caution leaders too much against an overuse of words, insulting the intelligence of the worshiper by telling him what he sees or exactly how he should feel with slide 3, for instance. If slide 3 has any "feeling" content, the worshipers will feel it. One should not be carried away by the fact that a captive audience is available. It will happen only once. Nowadays people in front of television sets are in the habit of turning certain commercial-laden programs off. Even if they don't leave, they'll walk out mentally and, of course, spiritually. Distractions such as turning lights up or down, moving near where attention is focused, getting up or down should always be avoided.

The worship leader can avoid holding a "jumpy" worship service whereby one visualizes a hymn by projecting slides, then turning the lights up for the scripture-reading, down for the next hymn, up for the prayer, and down for the next hymn. The audio-visual worship service calls for careful planning. One should arrange for a whole segment or portion to be visualized. If people are asked to pray when a picture signifying prayer or inducing us to pray is on the screen, they should be reminded that the worshipers are to use the picture to help lead them into the spirit and meaning of the prayer. The worship leader may say quietly, in the tone of an invitation, "While we continue looking at the picture, let us pray." The prayer may then be silent, or audible, or both.

Smoothness of operation helps insure a worshipful setting and mood. The theater uses soft lights, noiseless seats, ushers who know how to seat people. The church must not become theatrical, but it need not be undramatic and it can become proficient. The group of worshipers should be half ready when the prelude begins. The subdued lights will fade quickly (in church the organist should operate the rheostat) as the draperies are pulled and the first visual appears on the screen. If there are several persons involved in helping with the worship—leader, pianist, projectionist, and a person at the lights—the service should be carefully rehearsed so each person will know exactly what he is to do. It is better not to use bells, flashes of light, or those horrible words, "Next slide, please." Each assistant should have a complete script of the worship service.

One should work and plan for a smooth and well-ordered use of audio-visuals in worship. Every part of the service need not be visualized, though it is desirable on occasion to do so. The visuals used should be accurate and high-standard.

When attention is taken from Him whom one worships, the visual has got in the way. When the glamor of a film or an object, a flat picture, or a projected picture, gets in the way of a worshiper's giving glory to God, it should not be used.

The greatest misuse of audio-visuals has been in the area of worship. Too frequently audio-visual services of worship distract, and they are often disorganized. They attempt to do more than is possible. The leader usually operates, even if by lack of assumption, on the theory that this worship service is the last one in history. He includes every slide or every frame of a filmstrip or all the possible elements in worship.

There has been an overuse of heads of Christ, sunsets, and sunrises for all opening and closing frames of worship services. A service in which one always begins or ends with exactly the same visual leads nowhere. A benediction in the dark is far better than the tenth use of the same picture in the light. In fact the dark itself is an effective visual too, but take care in exploiting its use in worship.

The purpose and effect of an audio-visual worship service should not be vitiated or distorted by saccharine endings. A beautiful, flowing-haired head of Christ may be too soothing and too syrupy an ending to a worship service with a social action theme like "We Are All Brothers." The meaning of the cross should always be in every service, but there has been an overuse and sometimes a misuse of the cross.

The use of audio-visuals in worship tends to limit and to be illimitable. A worshiper may be stopped in his worshiping by the indiscriminate use of a visual, the wrong words with the right picture. Or a worshiper may be lifted as with wings to new heights where emotional conviction motivates him to register a new loyalty.

An uninspiring flat picture or slide will not lift the worshiper to new heights of aspiration. A disorganized series of pictures, whether slides or three frames from the end of a filmstrip, will distract and dilute what would otherwise be a vital encounter between man and God. The picture, moving or still, needs to be in keeping with the subject.

It is advisable not to break a train of thought or the mood of worship. The service should have unity. If the mood is properly established for the worshipful *viewing* of a film, the service should be completed on that same note. The leader of worship will not want to violate the spiritual sensibilities of sincere worshipers.

Criteria for Selection and Use

Technical Perfection. Be prepared. God is being worshiped. Man is not demonstrating his own genius or goodness.

Simplicity. Worship is deeper when the elements that comprise it are understood and appreciated. The frills may be saved for next Monday's magic show. People will be looking for them there.

Dignity. Worship is a dignified and holy act and should be led with dignity. The leader will seek to be neither pompous nor pious. He will be natural, conversational, worship-filled.

Beauty and Order. Worship can and should be beautiful. Something turns man to thoughts of God when he beholds the beautiful and the orderly. Something distracts when he hears an untuned piano, a disharmonious choir!

Truthfulness and Reality. One should use nothing false in the worship of God. Only the truth, the genuine thing will carry the mark of reality. Paper flowers, the use of copyright material without permission, camouflaging a picture and misinterpretation cannot lead to purity of worship.

Honesty. Every element of the service should be in keeping with what one believes about God.

Using a Flat Picture

For a family night at church the service of worship offers a good opportunity to use a flat picture.

THEME: A Loving Family

PURPOSE: To help the members of each family feel they are loved, to enlarge their conception of the function of each member; to learn God's will for their family living; and to be strengthened to do God's will.

AUDIO: Piano, voices of leader and group

VISUAL: Flat picture of Jesus learning at home

The picture, on an easel, should be well placed so that all ages may see, and well lighted with an inconspicuous spotlight. The room lights should be turned down slowly for the beginning. If the picture is small it can be "enlarged" by setting it against a larger plain background. No person's view of the visual should be obstructed.

ROOM ARRANGEMENT: Chairs should be placed so that all may see. The leader, facing the picture, remains seated throughout the service.

THE SERVICE OF WORSHIP

MUSIC: "O Jesus, Once a Nazareth Boy," played softly. Tune: "Seraph"

CALL TO WORSHIP

God is love. He loves fathers and mothers and boys and girls. Let us learn to love each other as we worship God, for God is love.

HYMN: "Tell Me the Stories of Jesus"

SCRIPTURE: Luke 2:39-48; 1 John 4:11-12, 16; 5:1-2

PICTURE INTERPRETATION: Factual information about the Holy Family is limited. We can imagine how they lived, how they loved each other. Joseph and Mary and Jesus were a loving family. Jesus studied with his mother; he helped his father. Together they shared many happy hours. Joseph and Mary and Jesus often went to where Joseph worked. Joseph loved his wife and son and wanted them near him. Mary liked to be near when her menfolk talked about important things like the synagogue school, the prophets, and the great people of Israel. The family liked to read from the scrolls, which were written in the Hebrew and the Aramaic languages. Jesus was quick to learn, and Mary and Joseph were good teachers. Mary knew that Jesus would soon finish his lesson and would want to help Joseph. Then he would want to eat and play.

Fathers and mothers teach us many things. They teach us to share in work and play. When parents and children love each other and share, they learn to become a loving, sharing family like the family of Jesus. When we learn how to love God we will learn how to love each other.

PRAYER: O God, our Father, we thank you for loving us. We thank you for the boy Jesus and for his father and mother. We are happy for our family. Forgive us when we do wrong and help us to look and listen for the best in others. As we look and listen, fill our eyes and ears with pictures of love and with noble thoughts. Keep us close to each other by helping us to learn as Jesus learned, to love as Jesus loved, to live as Jesus lived. In his name we pray. Amen.

SILENCE: (Let us think for a few moments about our family and remember how God loves each of us.)

HYMN: "For the Beauty of the Earth"

BENEDICTION: May the love of God go with each one of us. May we learn at home as Jesus did. May we, like Jesus, come to understand that God is love. May our family also become a loving family. Amen.

Using One Frame of a Filmstrip

A class or organization may wish to begin or close a program with a brief worship thought. In using one frame of a film-strip, it is best to have the screen and projector in place and to have persons ready to draw the shades unobtrusively. The group should know what is being done, which could be made known by an announcement before the service begins. Then the lights could be turned down and the picture projected. One should pause long enough for the group to "take in" the picture. Then the narration may be read.

A suitable and available picture should be chosen ahead of time. One could use frame 40, Part II of *Life of Christ*,[1] "The Great Commission" (Mark 16:15).

The disciples of Jesus had listened to the glad news, and they believed. And to Peter and James and John, and to all disciples, Jesus said, "Go into all the world and preach the gospel to the whole creation. And lo, I am with you always." Jesus' words were meant for us too. He wants us to go and serve him in all that we do. He is with us wherever we go.

Let us pray together the prayer of our Lord, "Our Father . . . and the glory forever." Amen.

Using Symbols

In a worship service for young people and adults symbols could be used effectively.

THEME: "Consecrated, Lord, to Thee"

PURPOSE: To acknowledge before God the work of every man; to recognize that all work in the interest of people is a high calling; to identify ourselves with all labor; to lift up the talent and skill of all workers before God and man and ask God's blessing upon all honest work.

---

[1] By Barosin. Produced by the Evangelical and Reformed Church.

AUDIO: Piano, voices of leader and group

VISUAL: A pick and shovel, preferably with clay or dirt clinging to them as though just used, may be placed against a contrasting background and illumined with an inconspicuous spotlight.

ROOM ARRANGEMENT: Chairs should be placed so that all may see. The leader, facing front, and the worshipers will remain seated throughout the service.

THE SERVICE OF WORSHIP

MUSIC: "O Master, Let Me Walk with Thee"

CALL TO WORSHIP

O come let us worship the Lord, in song, in word, in work. Let us come before God with tools of daily work. Let us worship God, remembering we are servants of Christ and brother to every man.

HYMN: "O Master Workman of the Race"

SCRIPTURE: Luke 2:51-52; Psalm 90:16-17; II Thessalonians 3:6-17

LITANY

Our Lord and Savior, Jesus Christ, knew work. For this, *We give God thanks.*

Jesus knew the weight of tools at close of day.
Praise God for tools.

He knew the worth of instruments that did the job.
Praise God for all such discernment.

His work and thought were one, all bound to build for God
and man.
Lord, bring unity and purpose to our thoughts and dreams.

For calloused hands and muscles strong,
We give thee thanks and sing a song of praise.

For rest that lifts the burdens of aching backs and weary feet,
We give God thanks.

For jobs well done and goals complete,
We give God thanks.

For work that disciplines our living,
May God be praised.

For work that makes us strong of heart, O God,
We ask a part.

For those whose work is low, or high, or in-between,
Unite us in a common cause.

And all those whose work serves others,
Make us to know them as brothers.

LEADER'S THOUGHTS *(to be altered or augmented to speak to the
needs of the worshipers)*
Tools touch the earth of which we are made.
God touches the earth, and man is more than clay.
Labor is good for man, for when directed aright it serves him
who works and him for whom the work is done.
Work is work, no matter where it is done or by whom.
Unless men dig, there can be no drainage of refuse,
There can be no bed-rock foundations,
No cornerstones,
No communities,

No joy,

No peace that comes from purpose served.

Unless men use their minds, their muscles,

Their minutes in service to others,

They are of no use to themselves.

Give thanks for a world of work;

For a chance to clean up a community,

To connect neighbors underground, or overhead, or on the earth itself,

To give heat and light and voice.

The digger of ditches is worthy of his hire.

He also serves.

Digging is a call from God, and those who dig will reach low to go high, reach out to go far.

The honest work of every man who serves his brother is an answer to the high calling of God.

Hymn Prayer: "Jesus, Thou Divine Companion"

Hymn: "My Master Was a Worker"

Benediction: Bless, O Lord, the labor of our hands. Bless those who benefit from whatever burdens we may bear. Bind us together with bonds of loving concern and compel us, by thy spirit brooding in our hearts, to accept a common cause with our brothers in Christ. Amen.

Using a Film in Worship

Worship is concerned with all of life. Any subject of concern to the Christian is subject matter about which man may hold conversation with God. The film used in worship will usually present the message or sermon. The remainder of the service will be built around the content of the film.

A film like *The Promise* by J. Arthur Rank would be selected for use at a time when one wanted to emphasize the reality of the Holy Spirit and interpret some of the ways in which certain persons believed the Holy Spirit worked. Worship lifts—it does not always explain. Worship exalts—it does not necessarily educate. Worship heals and tunes us in on power—it does not always solve or resolve.

A service of worship patterned after the following would lift, exalt, heal, and empower us.

PRELUDE: "Holy Spirit, Truth Divine"

CALL TO WORSHIP

"The Lord is in his holy temple; let all the earth keep silence before him. Do you not know that you are God's temple and that God's Spirit dwells in you?"

HYMN: "Spirit of God, Descend Upon My Heart"

SCRIPTURE: John 14:12-17

STATEMENT for the introduction of the film: Have you ever felt the presence of the Holy Spirit so strongly that you were stopped in your steps or in your thoughts? Have you ever had extra power from a source outside yourself?

There is such a power. A Mr. Townsend knew it, and so did the man appointed to take his place, the man who continued his work. "It is a power from on high . . . the promise of the Father."

THE FILM: (Following the showing of the film, keep the lights dimmed and close with—)

PRAYER: O God, our Father, we thank thee for the promise and the gift of the Holy Spirit. We have seen the work of the Holy Spirit. We have felt the power. Send thy Holy Spirit into our lives. Where there is need appoint us to the task. Enable us to accept the gift of power and the grace to strengthen and comfort others. "Breathe on us, breath of God, fill us with life anew." Amen.

(Turn the lights up slowly as the hymn is announced.)

Hymn: "Breathe on Me, Breath of God"

Benediction: May the peace of God, which passes all understanding, keep your hearts and minds in Christ Jesus this day and forevermore. Amen.

Bibliography

BOOKS AND PAMPHLETS

Audio-Visual Methods in Teaching by Edgar Dale. The Dryden Press. Revised 1954.

Projected Visual Aids in the Church by William S. Hockman. Pilgrim Press, 1947.

Visualizing the Curriculum by C. F. Hoban, C. F. Hoban, Jr., and S. B. Zisman. The Dryden Press, 1946.

Audio-Visual Materials: Their Nature and Use by Walter A. Wittich and Charles F. Schuller. Harper & Brothers, 1953.

Church Use of Audio-Visuals by Howard E. Tower. The Abingdon Press, 1950.

Look, Listen and Learn: A Manual on the Use of Audio-Visual Materials in Informal Education by L. H. Strauss and J. R. Kidd. Association Press, 1948.

Audio-Visual Resource Guide, Division of Christian Education, NCCCUSA.

The Gospel in Art by Albert Edward Bailey. The Pilgrim Press, 1944.

Christ and the Fine Arts by Cynthia Pearl Maus. Harper & Brothers, 1938.

Each with His Own Brush by Daniel Johnson Fleming. Friendship Press, 1952.

Audio-Visual Teaching Techniques by Frederick D. McClusky. Dubuque, Iowa, W. C. Brown, 1949.

Visual Aids in Fundamental Education, UNESCO publication distributed by Columbia University Press, 1952.

Here's How and When by Armilda B. Keiser. Friendship Press, 1952.

Marionettes: Easy to Make! Fun to Use! by Edith Flack Ackley. J. B. Lippincott.

Working with Juniors at Church by Dorothy La Croix Hill. The Abingdon Press.

Primary Children Learn at Church by Ethel L. Smither. The Abingdon Press.

Guiding Kindergarten Children in the Church School by Elizabeth McE. Shields. Revised by Dorothea G. Mallard. John Knox Press.

Aim Your Activities at Teaching Religion by Mrs. August Beck. Reprints of a series of articles on popular creative activities appearing in the *International Journal of Religious Education*, 1949-51.

Film Use in the Church by Parker, Stein, Vieth, Welker. Broadcasting and Film Commission, NCCCUSA.

How to Make Lantern Slides by G. E. Hamilton. Keystone View Company, 1940, (Illustrated. Free upon request.)

"Opaque Projection" A New Frontier in Teaching. American Optical Company, Chelsea, Massachusetts, 1941.

Manual for Training the Audio-Visual Counselor, Office of Audio-Visual Education, Board of Christian Education, Presbyterian Church, U.S.A.

PERIODICALS

Educational Screen and Audio-Visual Guide. 2000 Lincoln Park West, Chicago 14, Illinois. $4.00 a year.

Teaching Tools. 6327 Santa Monica Blvd., Los Angeles 38, California. $2.00 for four consecutive issues.